BCL- 3rded

ENGELS
ON
CAPITAL

YEARS
1924-1974

Frederick
ENGELS
ON
CAPITAL

| SYNOPSIS |
| REVIEWS |
| AND |
| SUPPLEMENTARY |
| MATERIAL. |

INTERNATIONAL PUBLISHERS
New York

Translated by Leonard E. Mins and originally
published in 1937 by International Publishers
—except for the *Forward* and the *Review for the
Rheinische Zeitung, 1867* which have been added
for this edition.

ISBN 0-7178-0408-9 (cloth); 0-7178-0409-7 (paperback)
Library of Congress Catalog Card Number 73-94192
© 1937, International Publishers Co., Inc.
© Renewed 1965, International Publishers Co., Inc.
Second Edition, 1974

Printed in the United States of America

PUBLISHER'S NOTE

With the exception of the review from the *Fortnightly Review* which was written in English, all Engels' writings in this book are translated from the German.

The page references enclosed in parentheses in the text are Engels' own from the first German edition of *Capital*. The page numbers enclosed in square brackets cross-reference these to the English edition, International Publishers, 1967.

CONTENTS

FOREWORD

The works collected here are but a small part of what
Engels wrote in connection with Marx's *Capital*. For over
half a century, Engels's creative activity was closely inter-
woven with that of Marx. The correspondence of the founders
of Marxism shows the extremely active share Engels had in
the elaboration of a number of the most important propositions of *Capital* and what a constant help he was to Marx
by his advice, his factual information and his critical remarks.
Many of Engels's works are devoted to the development and
substantiation of the basic propositions of the Marxian
doctrine. Engels's long years of personal collaboration with
Marx were followed by the enormous work of publishing
the last two volumes of *Capital* left by the author in
manuscript form, new editions of the first volume and
several other works by Marx. A number of prefaces written
by Engels to those of Marx's works which he published are
devoted to the defence of Marx's doctrine against its enemies.

* * *

The first part of the collection consists of *three reviews*
of the first volume of *Capital*. After the publication of the
first volume in 1867, one of the tasks of Marx and Engels
was to break the conspiracy of silence by which the bourgeoisie hoped to strangle at birth the doctrine which it hated.
A real conspiracy of silence had met the appearance in 1859
of Marx's work *A Contribution to the Critique of Political
Economy*. The first volume of *Capital* was threatened with
the same fate. Enormous efforts were displayed by Marx's
colleagues, and in the first place by Engels, to thwart that

plan. The working-class press was at the time exceedingly weak. Only in roundabout ways, through the general press, which was in the hands of the bourgeoisie, was it possible to arouse interest in the book among readers capable of helping spread the ideas it contained. Engels had to show extraordinary resourcefulness in order to overcome the mistrust of bourgeois editors. He wrote a number of reviews in a really Aesopian language as artful as that in which the Russian revolutionaries had to write in publications subjected to tsarist censorship. The class-spirited censorship of the bourgeois editors resulted in part of Engels's works not being published and part being distorted.

Three out of Engels's nine reviews of the first volume of *Capital* are printed in this collection. The *first* was printed in Nos. 12 and 13, March 21 and 28, 1868, of the *Demokratisches Wochenblatt (Democratic Weekly)*, a socialist publication appearing in Leipzig under the editorship of Wilhelm Liebknecht. The *second* was sent to the editor of the then progressive-bourgeois *Rheinische Zeitung,* by Marx's friend Kugelmann, who played a great part in organising reviews on *Capital;* the letter was not printed. The *third* review was written for the English *Fortnightly Review,* in which the progressive-minded Professor Beesly (chairman of the international meeting in London in 1864 at which the formation of the First International was proclaimed) had great influence. Engels signed this review with the name of his friend Samuel Moore. Only the first part of the article was written, the conclusion was to follow. However, the publisher and proprietor of the journal opposed the publication of the review and it never appeared.

The second part of the collection consists of the synopsis of the first volume of *Capital,* written by Engels. Engels took an active part in Marx's work on *Capital.* Marx sent him separate sheets of the first volume as they were printed, and Engels gave a detailed opinion on each chapter, each sheet. As soon as the first volume appeared, Engels undertook the work of summarising it. He wrote in a letter to Marx on April 17, 1868:

"I have a limited time at my disposal and the summarising of your book requires more work than I thought; after all, once having taken up the work, I must do it properly, and not only specially for the present purpose."

The "present purpose" referred to was apparently the writing of a review for the *Fortnightly Review*; however, a glance through the synopsis is sufficient to conclude that he really did the work "properly, and not only specially for the present purpose."

Engels had time to summarise only the first four chapters of the first volume of *Capital*. It must be borne in mind that in the first edition this volume was divided into six chapters which in subsequent editions were called parts, the fifth chapter being broken up into two parts, so that a total of seven parts resulted. The four chapters summarised by Engels therefore correspond to the first four parts of the first volume of *Capital* as it is now. It must further be borne in mind that Marx made a number of additions and alterations to the text in subsequent editions of *Capital*. In the first edition, for instance, Marx did not specially dwell in the first chapter, which is devoted to commodities, on the distinction between value and exchange-value as a form of it; a considerable part of the exposition of the form of value was given as an appendix at the end of the volume and was not included in Engels's synopsis.

The reviews and the synopsis made by Engels are inestimable aids to the study of *Capital*. The contents of *Capital* are given for the greater part in Marx's own words. The centre of gravity, in the synopsis as well as in the reviews, lies in the *theory of surplus-value*, the cornerstone of Marx's economic doctrine. Engels summarised Marx's theory of surplus-value with special care, characterising in detail the historical circumstances in which the relations of capitalist exploitation spread, the working class made its first steps in the struggle and the first skirmishes took place between labour and capital. Engels's synopsis is a great help in bringing out what is most fundamental; it fixes the reader's attention on the most important theoretical problems. Following Marx, Engels shows in his synopsis that the transition from one category to another is not a freak of reason but the reflection of the real historic process of development. Keeping to the order of Marx's exposition, he shows how, in the course of historic development, capital emerged on the basis of commodity production, how it subordinated to itself the whole of production, how simple co-operation was replaced by manufacture and this in turn by machine production. Engels also shows how the sharpening of the class contradictions immanent in capitalism and the capitalist use of machines leads to "the maturing of the elements of the overthrow of the old society and the establishment of a new one," that is, leads to the *socialist revolution of the proletariat.*

The third part of the collection is an essay intended as a supplement to the third volume of *Capital,* written by Engels in the last year of his life and published after his death. On Marx's behest, Engels completed the publication of *Capital* by putting out the second and third volumes, prepared and published the third and fourth editions of the first volume and afforded all possible assistance for translations in a number of languages. The third volume of *Capital* left the printers' in December 1894. Its appearance immediately provoked a lively literary polemic. The conspiracy of silence with which the bourgeoisie had met the appearance of *A Contribution to the Critique of Political Economy* and the first volume of *Capital* proved to be a useless weapon against Marxism in the nineties. The growth of the working-class movement and the rapid spread of the Marxian doctrine demanded of the bourgeoisie new methods of fighting. Engels followed all the press's reactions to the third volume of *Capital* with the utmost attention. Although suffering cruelly from the illness which soon led him to the grave, he did not give up his creative theoretical work. During the last weeks of his life, his pen put the last strokes to his brilliant "Supplement to *Capital,* Volume Three." Engels mentions this work in some of his letters. Writing to Kautsky on May 21, 1895, he informed him:

"Meanwhile I am about to send you a piece of work for *Neue Zeit* ... supplements and addenda to *Capital,* Book III, No. 1: Law of Value and Rate of Profit, reply to the doubts of Sombart and C. Schmidt. Later No. 2 will follow: the very considerably altered role of the Bourse since Marx wrote about it in 1865. To be continued according to demand and time available."

Engels managed to get but the first of these two parts ready for the press. Only a short summarised plan of the second, written by Engels for himself, has remained. The first part appeared in *Neue Zeit* soon after his death. The short synopsis "Alterations in the Function of the Exchange" was not made public until 1932.

Engels's article on the law of value and the rate of profit is an important addition to the third volume of *Capital* and is at the same time of considerable importance for the correct understanding of the Marxian economic theory as a whole. Countless critics of Marx used up mountains of paper trying to prove the alleged contradiction between the first and the third volumes of *Capital*. In his article Engels exposed the avowed enemies of Marxism as well as those who clothed themselves in the apparel of "friends" of Marxism and who reduced value to "a logical fact" (W. Sombart), or to "a theoretically indispensable fiction" (C. Schmidt). Proceeding from Marx's proposition that value, not only theoretically but also historically, is the *prius* (antecedent) of the price of production, Engels shows the historical appearance of value with the rise and development of exchange, and the historical transition from value to prices of production when simple commodity production was superseded by capitalism.

The especial value of this essay lies in its giving a concise and clear characteristic of the nature of simple commodity production and the process of transition from that type of production to capitalism. Engels shows the law of value as the *law of motion* of commodity production. He underlines the exceptional length of the epoch during which the law of value is effective. He traces the rise of capitalist relations in a number of actual historic examples and proves how these relations seize on the domain of production. Engels's essay is a splendid model of the genuine materialist explanation of the Marxian theory of value; and is still unsurpassed as a weapon in the fight against all kinds of idealistic distortions of Marxism.

As was said above, the second part of this, Engels's last work on economics, remained only in the form of an elaborate plan. In it Engels sets himself the task of outlining the changes and evolutions in capitalist economy during the last third of the nineteenth century.

Those decades were the period of transition from the old capitalism of the epoch of free competition to imperialism—monopoly capitalism, which is characterised by the gigantic growth and sharpening of the contradictions of the bourgeois system. A Marxist study of imperialism as the highest phase of capitalism was given by Lenin, who continued the work of Marx and Engels and raised Marxism to a new and higher stage. Basing himself on Marx's study of the fundamental laws of the development of capitalist production given in *Capital*, Lenin formulated the theory of imperialism as the new and last stage of capitalism, disclosed the contradictions and ulcers that are eating it away, and demonstrated the inevitability of its downfall and the victory of the proletarian revolution.

Engels could not give the characteristics of the new his-·torical stage in the development of capitalism, as he did not live to see the time in which it completely took shape. In his draft article on the Exchange he simply points out some of the new phenomena in the economy of capitalist countries, without raising the question of a new stage in the development of capitalism. He noted the spread of joint-stock forms of enterprises, the transformation of individual enterprises into joint-stock companies, the concentration and amalgamation of enterprises in whole branches, and, finally, the appearance of monopolies. As an example of big monopoly he recalls the English United Alkali Trust with its capital of £6,000,000 which was enormous for the time. Engels's editorial insertion in Chapter 27 of Volume III of *Capital* also deals with the monopolies; it is given as an appendix to the present collection. In the two concluding points of his plan Engels raises the problem of the export of capital and the division of the colonial world.

Institute of Marxism-Leninism
under the Central Committee
of the Communist Party
of the Soviet Union

I
REVIEWS
ON *CAPITAL*,
VOLUME ONE

MARX'S *CAPITAL*[1]

I

As long as there have been capitalists and workers on earth, no book has appeared which is of as much importance for the workers as the one before us. The relation between capital and labour, the hinge on which our entire present system of society turns, is here treated scientifically for the first time and with a thoroughness and acuity possible only for a German. Valuable as the writings of an Owen, Saint-Simon, Fourier are and will remain, it was reserved for a German first to climb to the height from which the whole field of modern social relations can be seen clearly and in full view just as the lower mountain scenery is seen by an observer standing on the topmost peak.

Political economy up to now has taught us that labour is the source of all wealth and the measure of all values, so that two objects whose production has cost the same labour-time possess the same value and must also be exchanged for each other, since on the average only equal values are exchangeable for one another. At the same time, however, it teaches that there exists a kind of stored-up labour which it calls capital; that this capital, owing to the auxiliary sources contained in it, raises the productivity of living labour a hundred and a thousandfold, and in return claims a certain compensation which is termed profit or gain. As we all know, this occurs in reality in such a way that the profits of stored-up, dead labour become ever more

---

[1] Appeared in the Leipzig *Demokratisches Wochenblatt*, Nos. 12 and 13, March 21 and 28, 1868.—*Ed.*

massive, the capital of the capitalists becomes ever more colossal, while the wages of living labour constantly decrease, and the mass of workers living solely on wages grows ever more numerous and poverty-stricken. How is this contradiction to be solved? How can there remain a profit for the capitalist if the worker gets back the full value of the labour he adds to his product? And yet this should be the case, since only equal values are exchanged. On the other hand, how can equal values be exchanged, how can the worker receive the full value of his product, if, as is admitted by many economists, this product is divided between him and the capitalist? Economics up to now has been helpless in the face of this contradiction and writes or stutters embarrassed meaningless phrases. Even the previous socialist critics of economics were unable to do more than emphasise the contradiction; no one has solved it, until now at last Marx has traced the process by which this profit arises right to its birthplace and has thereby made everything clear.

In tracing the development of capital, Marx starts from the simple, notoriously obvious fact that the capitalists turn their capital to account by exchange: they buy commodities for their money and afterwards sell them for more money than they cost them. For example, a capitalist buys cotton for 1,000 talers and then sells it for 1,100, thus "earning" 100 talers. This excess of 100 talers over the original capital Marx calls *surplus-value*. Where does this surplus-value come from? According to the economists' assumption, only equal values are exchanged, and in the sphere of abstract theory this is correct. Hence, the purchase of cotton and its subsequent sale can just as little yield surplus-value as the exchange of a silver taler for thirty silver groschen and the re-exchange of the small coins for a silver taler, a process by which one becomes neither richer nor poorer. But surplus-value can just as little arise from sellers selling commodities above their value, or buyers buying them below their value, because each one is in turn buyer and seller and this would, therefore, again balance. No more can it arise from buyers and sellers reciprocally overreaching each other, for this would create no new or surplus-value, but would only distribute the existing capital differently between the capitalists. In spite of the fact that the capitalist buys

14

the commodities at their value and sells them at their value, he gets more value out than he put in. How does this happen?

Under present social conditions the capitalist finds on the commodity market a *commodity* which has the peculiar property that *its use is a source of new value, is a creation of new value.* This commodity is *labour-power.*

What is the value of labour-power? The value of every commodity is measured by the labour required for its production. Labour-power exists in the shape of the living worker who needs a definite amount of means of subsistence for himself and for his family, which ensures the continuance of labour-power even after his death. Hence the labour-time necessary for producing these means of subsistence represents the value of labour-power. The capitalist pays him weekly and thereby purchases the use of one week's labour of the worker. So far Messrs. the economists will pretty well agree with us as to the value of labour-power.

The capitalist now sets his worker to work. In a certain time the worker will have delivered as much labour as was represented by his weekly wage. Supposing that the weekly wage of a worker represents three labour days, then, if the worker begins on Monday he has by Wednesday evening *replaced* for the capitalist *the full value of the wage paid.* But does he then stop working? By no means. The capitalist has bought his *week's* labour and the worker must go on working during the last three days of the week too. This *surplus-labour* of the worker, over and above the time necessary to replace his wage, is the *source of surplus-value,* of profit, of the continually growing accumulation of capital.

Do not say it is an arbitrary assumption that the worker earns in three days the wages he has received and works the remaining three days for the capitalist. Whether he takes exactly three days to replace his wages, or two or four, is, of course, quite immaterial here and depends upon circumstances; the main point is that the capitalist, besides the labour he pays for, also extracts labour that he *does not pay for;* and this is no arbitrary assumption, for if the capitalist extracted from the worker over a long period only as much labour as he paid him for in wages, he would shut down his workshops, since indeed his whole profit would come to nought.

Here we have the solution of all those contradictions. The origin of surplus-value (of which the capitalist's profit forms an important part) is now quite clear and natural. The value of the labour-power is paid for, but this value is far less than that which the capitalist can extract from the labour-power, and it is precisely the difference, the *unpaid labour*, that constitutes the share of the capitalist, or more accurately, of the capitalist class. For even the profit that the cotton dealer made on his cotton in the above example must consist of unpaid labour, if cotton prices have not risen. The trader must have sold it to a cotton manufacturer, who is able to extract from his product a profit for himself besides the original 100 talers, and therefore shares with him the unpaid labour he has pocketed. In general, it is this unpaid labour which maintains all the non-working members of society. The state and municipal taxes, as far as they affect the capitalist class, the rent of the landowners, etc., are paid from it. On it rests the whole existing social system.

It would be absurd to assume that unpaid labour arose only under present conditions, where production is carried on by capitalists on the one hand and wage-workers on the other. On the contrary, the oppressed class at all times has had to perform unpaid labour. During the whole long period when slavery was the prevailing form of the organisation of labour, the slaves had to perform much more labour than was returned to them in the form of means of subsistence. The same was the case under the rule of serfdom and right up to the abolition of peasant *corvée* labour; here in fact the difference stands out palpably between the time during which the peasant works for his own maintenance and the surplus-labour for the feudal lord, precisely because the latter is carried out separately from the former. The form has now been changed, but the substance remains and as long as "a part of society possesses the monopoly of the means of production, the labourer, free or not free, must add to the working-time necessary for his own maintenance an extra working-time in order to produce the means of subsistence for the owners of the means of production." (202 [235].)

In the previous article we saw that every worker employed by the capitalist performs a twofold labour: during one part of his working-time he replaces the wages advanced to him by the capitalist, and this part of his labour Marx terms *necessary labour*. But afterwards he has to go on working and during that time he produces *surplus-value* for the capitalist, a significant portion of which constitutes profit. That part of the labour is called *surplus-labour*.

Let us assume that the worker works three days of the week to replace his wages and three days to produce surplus-value for the capitalist. Putting it otherwise, it means that with a twelve-hour working-day he works six hours daily for his wages and six hours for the production of surplus-value. One can get only six days out of the week, seven at most, even by including Sunday, but one can extract six, eight, ten, twelve, fifteen or even more hours of labour out of every working-day. The worker sells the capitalist a working-day for his day's wages. But, *what is a working-day?* Eight hours or eighteen?

It is in the capitalist's interest to make the working-day as long as possible. The longer it is, the more surplus-value is produced. The worker correctly feels that every hour of labour which he performs over and above the replacement of his wage is unjustly taken from him; he experiences with his own body what it means to work excessive hours. The capitalist fights for his profit, the worker for his health, for a few hours of daily rest, to be able, as a human being, to have other occupations than working, sleeping and eating. It may be remarked in passing that it does not depend at all upon the good will of the individual capitalists whether they desire to embark on this struggle or not, since competition compels even the most philanthropic among them to join with his colleagues and to make a working-time as long as theirs the rule.

The struggle for the fixing of the working-day has lasted from the first appearance of free workers in history up to the present day. In various trades different traditional working-days prevail, but in reality they are seldom observed. Only where the law fixes the working-day and supervises its observance can one really say that there exists a normal working-day. And up to now this is the case almost exclusively in the factory districts of England. Here the ten-hour working-day (ten-and-a-half hours on five days, seven-and-a-half hours on Saturday) has been fixed for all women and for youths of thirteen to eighteen; and since the men cannot work without them, they also come under the ten-hour working-day. This law has been won by English factory workers through years of endurance, through the most persistent, stubborn struggle with the factory owners, through freedom of the press, the right of association and assembly, and also through adroit utilisation of the divisions within the ruling class itself. It has become the palladium of the English workers; it has gradually been extended to all important branches of industry and last year to almost *all trades*, at least to all those in which women and children are employed. The present work contains most exhaustive material on the history of this legislative regulation of the working-day in England. The next "North-German Reichstag" will also have factory regulations, and therefore the regulation of factory labour, to discuss. We expect that none of the deputies elected by German workers will go to discuss this bill without previously making themselves thoroughly conversant with *Marx's* book. *Much can be achieved there.* The divisions within the ruling classes are more favourable to the workers than they ever were in England, because *universal suffrage compels the ruling classes to court the favour of the workers.* Four or five representatives of the proletariat are *a power* under these circumstances, if they know how to use their position, if above all they know what is at issue, which the bourgeois do not know. And Marx's book gives them in ready form all the material required for this.

We will pass over a number of other very fine investigations of more theoretical interest and come to the final chapter which deals with the accumulation of capital. Here it is first shown that the capitalist mode of production, *i.e.*, that which presupposes capitalists on the one hand and wage-workers on the other, not only continually reproduces the capital of the capitalist, but also continually reproduces the poverty of the workers at the same time; so that it is ensured that there always exist anew, on the one hand, capitalists who are the owners of all means of subsistence, raw materials and instruments of labour, and, on the other, the great mass

18

of workers who are compelled to sell their labour-power to these capitalists for an amount of the means of subsistence which at best just suffices to maintain them capable of working and to bring up a new generation of able-bodied proletarians. But capital is not merely reproduced; it is continually increased and multiplied—and so is its power over the propertyless class of workers. And just as capital itself is reproduced on an ever-greater scale, so the modern capitalist mode of production reproduces the class of propertyless workers also on an ever-greater scale and in ever-greater numbers. "... Accumulation [of capital] reproduces the capital-relation on a progressive scale, more capitalists or larger capitalists at this pole, more wage-workers at that. ... *Accumulation of capital is, therefore, increase of the proletariat.*" (600 [613].) Since, however, owing to the progress of machinery, owing to improved agriculture, etc., fewer and fewer workers are necessary in order to produce the same quantity of products, since this perfecting, *i.e.,* this making the workers superfluous, grows more rapidly than capital itself, what becomes of this ever-increasing number of workers? They form an industrial reserve army, which, during times of bad or moderate business, is paid *below* the value of its labour and is irregularly employed, or comes under the care of public Poor Law institutions, but which is indispensable to the capitalist class at times when business is especially lively, as is palpably evident in England—and which *under all circumstances* serves to break the power of resistance of the regularly employed workers and to keep their wages down. "The greater the social wealth ... the greater is the [relative surplus-population or][1] industrial reserve army. ... But the greater this reserve army in proportion to the active [regularly employed] labour army, the greater is the mass of a consolidated [permanent] surplus-population [or strata of workers] whose misery is in inverse ratio to its torment of labour. The more extensive, finally, the Lazarus-layers of the working class, and the industrial reserve army, the greater is official pauperism. *This is the absolute general law of capitalist accumulation.*" (631 [644].)

These, strictly scientifically proved—and the official economists take great care not to make even an attempt at refu-

---

[1] Insertions in brackets by Engels.—*Ed.*

tation—are some of the chief laws of the modern, capitalist social system. But with this is everything said? By no means. Just as sharply as Marx stresses the bad sides of capitalist production, does he also clearly prove that this social form was necessary to develop the productive forces of society to a level which will make possible an equal development, worthy of human beings, for *all* members of society. All earlier forms of society were too poor for this. Capitalist production for the first time creates the wealth and the productive forces necessary for this, but at the same time it also creates in the mass of oppressed workers the social class which is more and more compelled to claim the utilisation of this wealth and these productive forces for the whole of society—instead of as today for a monopolist class.

KARL MARX, *DAS KAPITAL*
KRITIK DER POLITISCHEN OEKONOMIE

I BAND: DER PRODUKTIONSPROZESS
DES KAPITALS

Hamburg, Otto Meissner, 1867.[1]

Universal suffrage has added to the already existing parliamentary parties a new one, the Social-Democratic Party. In the last elections to the North-German Reichstag it nominated its own candidates in most large towns, in all factory districts, and six or eight of its deputies were returned. In comparison with the last election but one it has developed considerably greater strength and it can therefore be assumed that, for the present at least, it is still growing. It would be folly to wish to continue to pass over in splendid silence the existence, activity and doctrines of such a party in a country in which universal suffrage has laid the final decision in the hands of the most numerous and poorest class.

However divided and unsettled the few Social-Democratic deputies may be among themselves, it can be assumed with assurance that all groups of that party will welcome the present book as their *theoretical bible*, the arsenal from which they will draw their most substantial arguments. On these grounds alone the book deserves particular attention. But its contents too are such as will arouse interest. Whereas Lassalle's main argumentation—and in political economy Lassalle was but a disciple of Marx—is confined to continual repetition of Ricardo's so-called wages law, we have before us a work which treats the whole relation of capital and labour in its connection with the whole of economic science with indisputably rare erudition and which sets as its ultimate aim *"to lay bare the economic law of motion of modern*

---

[1] Written for the *Rheinische Zeitung* in October 1867. Remained unpublished. —*Ed.*

society", and thereby, after obviously sincere investigations carried out with unmistakable knowledge of the subject, comes to the conclusion that the whole "capitalist mode of production" must be abolished. We should, however, like further to draw attention to the fact that, apart from the conclusions, the author in the course of his work presents quite a number of the major points of economics in a completely new light and in purely scientific questions arrives at results which are greatly at variance with current economics and which orthodox economists must seriously criticise and scientifically refute if they do not wish to see the doctrine they have so far professed founder. In the interest of science it is desirable that a polemic should develop very soon in specialised journals precisely on these points.

Marx begins by expounding the relation between commodity and money, the most essential of which was already published some time ago in a special work. Then he goes on to capital and here we have the cardinal point of the whole work. What is capital? Money which is changed into a commodity in order to be changed back from a commodity into more money than the original sum. When I buy cotton for 100 talers and sell it for 110 talers I preserve my 100 talers as capital, value which expands itself. Now the question arises: where do the 10 talers which I gain in this process come from? How does it happen that as a result of two simple exchanges 100 talers becomes 110. For economics presupposes that in all exchanges equal values are exchanged. Marx then considers all possible cases (fluctuation in prices of commodities, etc.) in order to prove that in the conditions assumed by economics the creation of 10 talers *surplus-value* out of the original 100 talers is *impossible.* Yet this process takes place daily and the economists have not yet given us an explanation for it. Marx provides the following explanation: the puzzle can be solved only if we find on the market a commodity of a quite peculiar kind, a commodity whose use-value consists in producing exchange-value. This commodity exists—it is *labour-power.* The capitalist buys labour-power on the market and makes it work for him in order in turn to sell its product. So we must first of all investigate labour-power.

What is the value of labour-power? According to the generally known law, it is the value of the means of subsistence necessary to maintain and procreate the labourer in the way established in a given country and a given historical epoch. We assume that the labourer is paid the entire value of his labour-power. Further we assume that this value is represented by *six* hours' work daily, or *half* a working-day. But the capitalist asserts that he has bought labour-power for *a whole* working-day and he makes the labourer work twelve hours or more. With a twelve-hour working-day he therefore acquires the product of six hours' work without paying for it. From this Marx concludes: *all surplus-value*, no matter how it is divided, as profit of the capitalist, ground-rent, taxes, etc., is *unpaid labour*.

From the manufacturer's interest to extract as much unpaid labour as possible every day and the contrary interest of the labourer arises the struggle over the length of the working-day. In an illustration which is very much worth reading and which takes up about a hundred pages, Marx describes the origin of this struggle in English modern industry which, in spite of the protests of the free-trade manufacturers, ended last spring in not only factory industry but all small establishments and even all domestic industry being subjected to the restrictions of the Factory Act, according to which the maximum working-day for women and children under eighteen —and thereby indirectly for men too in the most important branches of industry—was fixed at $10^{1}/_{2}$ hours. At the same time he explains why English industry did not suffer, but on the contrary gained thereby, as the work of each individual won more in intensity than it lost in duration.

But there is another way of increasing surplus-value besides lengthening the working-day beyond the time required for the production of the necessary means of subsistence or their value. A given working-day, let us say of twelve hours, includes, according to our previous assumption, six hours of necessary work and six hours used for the production of surplus-value. If a means is found to cut the necessary working-time down to five hours, seven hours remain during which surplus-value will be produced. This can be achieved by a reduction in the working-time required to produce the necessary means of subsistence, in other words by cheapening the means of subsistence, and this in turn only by improving production. On this point Marx again gives a detailed illustration by investigating or describing the three main levers by which these improvements are brought about: 1) *co-opera-tion*, or multiplication of power, which results from the simultaneous and systematic joint work of a number of workers; 2) *division of labour*, as it took shape in the period of manufacture proper (*i.e.*, up to about 1770); finally 3) *machinery* by the help of which modern industry has since developed. These descriptions are also of great interest and show astonishing knowledge of the subject even down to technological details.

We cannot enter into further details of the investigation on surplus-value and wages; we merely note, in order to avoid misunderstandings, that, as Marx proves by a number of quotations, orthodox economics is not unaware of the fact that wages are less than the whole product of work. It is to be hoped that this book will provide Messrs. the orthodox economists with the opportunity of giving us closer explanations on this really surprising point. It will be appreciated that all the factual proofs that Marx gives are taken from the best sources, mostly official parliamentary reports. We take this opportunity of supporting the suggestion, made indirectly by the author in the Preface, that in Germany too a thorough inquiry into the condition of the workers in the various industries be made by government officials—who, however, must not be prejudiced bureaucrats—and that the reports be submitted to the Reichstag and the public.

The first volume ends with a study of the accumulation of capital. This point has often been written about, although we must admit that here too much of what is given is new and that light is shed on the old from new sides. The most original is the attempted proof that side by side with the concentration and accumulation of capital, and in step with it, the accumulation of a surplus working population is going on, and that both together will in the end make a social upheaval necessary, on the one hand, and possible on the other.

Whatever opinion the reader may have of the author's socialist views, we think that we have shown him that he is here in presence of a work which stands well above the usual Social-Democratic publications. To that we add that with the exception of the strongly dialectical things on the first 40 pages, the book, in spite of all its scientific rigour, is very easy to understand and because of the author's sarcastic manner, which spares no one, is even interestingly written.

094324

KARL MARX ON CAPITAL[1]

Mr. Thomas Tooke, in his inquiries on currency, points out the fact that money, in its function as capital, undergoes a reflux to its point of issue, while this is not the case with money performing the function of mere currency. This distinction (which, however, had been established long before by Sir James Steuart) is used by Mr. Tooke merely as a link in his argumentation against the "Currency men" and their assertions as to the influence of the issue of paper money on the prices of commodities. Our author, on the contrary, makes this distinction the starting point of his inquiry into the nature of capital itself, and especially as regards the question: How is money, this independent form of existence of value, converted into capital?

All sorts of businessmen—says Turgot—have this in common, that they *buy in order to sell*; their purchases are an advance which afterwards is returned to them.

To buy in order to sell, such is indeed the transaction in which money functions as capital, and which necessitates its return to its point of issue; in contradistinction to *selling in order to buy*, in which process money *may* function as currency only. Thus it is seen that the different order in which the acts of selling and buying follow upon each other, impresses upon money two different motions of circulation. In order to illustrate these two processes, our author gives the following formulae:

To sell in order to buy: a commodity C is exchanged for money M, which is again exchanged for another commodity C; or: $C-M-C$.

---

[1] Written for the *Fortnightly Review* in June 1868, remained unpublished.—*Ed.*

To buy in order to sell: money is exchanged for a commodity and this is again exchanged for money: $M-C-M$.

The formula $C-M-C$ represents the simple circulation of commodities, in which money functions as means of circulation, as currency. This formula is analysed in the first chapter of our book which contains a new and very simple theory of value and of money, extremely interesting scientifically, but which we here leave out of consideration as, on the whole, immaterial to what we consider the vital points of Mr. Marx's views on capital.

The formula $M-C-M$, on the other hand, represents that form of circulation in which money resolves itself into capital.

The process of buying in order to sell: $M-C-M$, may evidently be resolved into $M-M$; it is an indirect exchange of money against money. Suppose I buy cotton for £1,000 and sell it for £1,100; then, *in fine*, I have exchanged £1,000 for £1,100, money for money.

Now, if this process were always to result in returning to me the same sum of money which I had advanced, it would be absurd. But, whether the merchant, who had advanced £1,000, realises £1,100, or £1,000, or even £900 only, his money has gone through a phase essentially different from that of the formula $C-M-C$; which formula means, to sell in order to buy, to sell what you do not want in order to be able to buy that what you do want. Let us compare the two formulae.

Each process is composed of two phases or acts, and these two acts are identical in both formulae; but there is a great difference between the two processes themselves. In $C-M-C$, money is merely the mediator; the commodity, useful value, forms the starting and the concluding point. In $M-C-M$, the commodity is the intermediate link, while money is the beginning and the end. In $C-M-C$ the money is spent once for all; in $M-C-M$ it is merely advanced, with the intention to recover it; it returns to its point of issue, and in this we have a first palpable difference between the circulation of money as *currency* and of money as *capital*.

In the process of selling in order to buy, $C-M-C$, the money can return to its point of issue on the condition only that the whole process be repeated, that a fresh quantity of commodity be sold. The reflux, therefore, is independent of the process itself. But in $M-C-M$, this reflux is a necessity and intended from the beginning; if it does not take place, there is a hitch somewhere and the process remains incomplete.

To sell in order to buy, has for its object the acquisition of *useful* value; to buy in order to sell, that of *exchangeable* value.

In the formula $C-M-C$, the two extremes are, economically speaking, identical. They are both commodities; they are, moreover, of the same quantitative value, for the whole theory of value implies the supposition that, normally, equivalents only are exchanged. At the same time, these two extremes $C-C$ are two useful values different in quality, and they are exchanged on that very account. In process of $M-C-M$, the whole operation, at the first glance, appears meaningless. To exchange £100 for £100, and that by a roundabout process, appears absurd. A sum of money can differ from another sum of money by its quantity only. $M-C-M$, therefore, can only have any meaning by the quantitative difference of its extremes. There must be more money drawn out from circulation than had been thrown into it. The cotton bought for £1,000 is sold for £1,100=£1,000+£100; the formula representing the process, thus, changes to $M-C-M'$, in which $M'=M+\triangle M$, M plus an increment. This $\triangle M$, this increment, Mr. Marx calls *surplus-value*.[1] The value originally advanced not only maintains itself, it also adds to itself an increment, it *begets value,* and *it is this process which changes money into capital.*

In the form of circulation $C-M-C$, the extremes *may,* certainly, also differ in value, but such a circumstance would here be perfectly indifferent; the formula does not become absurd if both extremes are equivalents. On the contrary, it is a condition of its normal character that they should be so.

The repetition of $C-M-C$ is limited by circumstances entirely extraneous to the process of exchange itself: by the requirements of consumption. But in $M-C-M$, beginning and end are identical as to quality, and by that very fact the motion is, or may be, perpetual. No doubt, $M+\triangle M$ is different in quantity from M; but still it is a mere limited sum of money. If you spend it, it will cease to be capital; if

---

[1] Wherever *value* is here used without qualification, it always means *value in exchange.*

you withdraw it from circulation, it will be a stationary hoard. The inducement once admitted for the process of making value beget value, this inducement exists as much for M' as it existed for M; the motion of capital becomes perpetual and endless, because at the close of each separate transaction its end is no more attained than before. The performance of this endless process transforms the owner of money into a *capitalist*.

Apparently, the formula $M-C-M$ is applicable to merchants' capital alone. But the manufacturers' capital, too, is money which is exchanged for commodities and re-exchanged for more money. No doubt, in this case, a number of operations intervene between purchase and sale, operations which are performed outside of the sphere of mere circulation; but they do not change anything in the nature of the process. On the other hand, we see the same process in its most abbreviated form in capital lent on interest. Here the formula dwindles down to $M-M'$, value which is, so to say, greater than itself.

But whence does this increment of M, this surplus-value arise? Our previous inquiries into the nature of commodities, of value, of money, and of circulation itself, not only leave it unexplained, but appear even to exclude any form of circulation which results in such a thing as a surplus-value. The whole difference between the circulation of commodities $(C-M-C)$ and the circulation of money as capital $(M-C-M)$ appears to consist in a simple reversion of the process; how should this reversion be capable of producing such a strange result?

Moreover: this reversion exists only for *one* of the three parties to the process. I, as a capitalist, buy a commodity from A, and sell it again to B. A and B appear as mere sellers and buyers of commodities. I myself appear, in buying from A, merely as an owner of money, and in selling to B, as owner of a commodity; but in neither transaction do I appear as a capitalist, as the representative of something which is *more* than either money or commodity. For A the transaction began with a sale, for B it began with a purchase. If from my point of view there is a reversion of the formula $C-M-C$, there is none from theirs. Besides, there is nothing to prevent A from selling his commodity to B without my intervention, and then there would be no occasion for any surplus-value.

Suppose *A* and *B* buy their respective requirements from each other directly. As far as useful value is concerned they may both be gainers. *A* may even be able to produce more of his particular commodity than *B* could produce in the same time, and *vice versa*, in which case they both would gain. But it is different with regard to value in exchange. In this latter case equal quantities of value are exchanged, whether money serves as the medium or not.

Considered in the abstract, that is to say excluding all circumstances which are not deducible from the inherent laws of the simple circulation of commodities, there is in this simple circulation, besides the fact of one useful value being replaced by another, a mere change of form of the commodity. *The same* value in exchange, the same quantity of social labour fixed in an object, remains in the hands of the owner of the commodity, be it in the shape of this commodity itself, or in that of the money it is sold for, or in that of the second commodity bought for the money. This change of form does not in any way involve any change in the quantity of the value, as little as the exchange of a five pound note for five sovereigns. Inasmuch as there is merely a change in the *form* of the value in exchange, there must be exchange of equivalents, at least whenever the process takes place in its purity and under normal conditions. Commodities *may* be sold at prices above or below their values, but if they are, the law of the exchange of commodities is always violated. In its pure and normal form, therefore, the exchange of commodities is not a means of creating surplus-value. Hence arises the error of all economists who attempt to derive surplus-value from the exchange of commodities, such as Condillac.

We will, however, suppose, that the process does not take place under normal conditions, and that non-equivalents are exchanged. Let every seller, for instance, sell his commodity 10 per cent above its value. *Caeteris paribus* everybody loses again as a buyer what he has gained as a seller. It would be exactly the same as if the value of money had fallen 10 per cent. The reverse, with the same effect, would take place if all buyers bought their goods 10 per cent below their value. We do not get an inch nearer to a solution by supposing that every owner of commodities sells them above their value in his quality as a producer and buys them above their value in his quality as a consumer.

The consistent representatives of the delusion that surplus-value arises from a nominal addition to the price of commodities presuppose always the existence of a class which buys without ever selling, which consumes without producing. At this stage of our inquiry, the existence of such a class is as yet inexplicable. But admit it. Whence does that class receive the money with which it keeps buying? Evidently from the producers of commodities—on the strength of no matter what legal or compulsory titles, without exchange. To sell, to such a class, commodities above their value, means nothing but to recover a portion of the money which has been given away gratuitously. Thus the cities of Asia Minor, while paying a tribute to the Romans, recovered part of this money by cheating the Romans in trade; but after all, these cities were the greatest losers of the two. This, then, is no method of creating surplus-value.

Let us suppose the case of cheating. A sells to B wine of the value of £40 for corn of the value of £50. A has gained £10 and B has lost £10, but betwixt them, they have only £90 just as before. Value has been transferred but not created. The whole capitalist class of a country cannot, by cheating one another, increase their collective wealth.

Therefore: If equivalents are exchanged, there arises no surplus-value, and if non-equivalents are exchanged, there arises no surplus-value either. The circulation of commodities creates no new value. This is the reason why the two oldest and most popular forms of capital, commercial capital and interest-bearing capital, are here left entirely out of consideration. To explain the surplus-value appropriated by these two forms of capital otherwise than as the result of mere cheating, a number of intermediate links are required which are still wanting at this stage of the inquiry. Later on we shall see that they both are secondary forms only and shall also trace the cause why both appear in history long before modern capital.

Surplus-value, then, cannot originate from the circulation of commodities. But can it originate outside of it? Outside of it, the owner of a commodity is simply the producer of that commodity, the value of which is established by the amount of his labour contained in it and measured by a fixed social law. This value is expressed in money of account, say, in a price of £10. But this price of £10 is not at the

30

same time a price of £11; this labour contained in the commodity creates value, but no value which begets new value; it can add new value to existing value, but merely by adding new labour. How, then, should the owner of a commodity, outside the sphere of circulation, without coming into contact with other owners of commodities—how should he be able to produce surplus-value, or in other words, to change commodities or money into capital?

"Capital, then, cannot originate from the circulation of commodities, and no more can it *not* originate from it. It has to find its source in it, and yet *not* in it. The change of money into capital has to be explained on the basis of the laws inherent to the exchange of commodities, *the exchange of equivalents forming the starting-point.* Our owner of money, as yet the mere chrysalis of a capitalist, has to buy his commodities at their value, to sell them at their value, and yet to extract more money[1] from this process than he has invested in it. His development into the capitalist butterfly has to take place within the sphere of the circulation of commodities, and yet *not* within it. These are the terms of the problem. *Hic Rhodus, hic salta.*"[2] [Pp. 165-66.]

And now for the solution:

"The change in the value of the money which is to be transformed into capital, cannot take place in that money itself; for, as means of purchase and means of payment, it merely *realises* the price of the commodity which it buys or pays for, while if it remained in its money-form, without being exchanged, it could never change its value at all. No more can the change arise from the second act of the process, the re-sale of the commodity; because this merely changes the commodity from its natural form into the form of money. *The change must take place with the commodity* which is bought in the first act *M—C;* but it cannot take place in its value in exchange, because we exchange equivalents; the commodity is bought at its value. *The change can only arise from its value in use,* that is *from the use which is made of it.* In order to extract value in exchange from the use of a commodity, our owner of money must have the good luck

---

[1] In *Capital,* value *(Wert).—Ed.*
[2] In this review, all quotations from *Capital,* Vol. I, were translated into English by Engels.—*Ed.*

to discover, within the sphere of circulation, in the market, a commodity, *the useful value of which is endowed with the peculiar quality of being a source of exchangeable value, the using-up of which is the realisation of labour and therefore the creation of value.* And the owner of money finds, in the market, such a specific commodity: the power to work, *the labour-power.*

"By power to work, or labour-power, we understand the sum-total of the physical and mental faculties which exist in the living person of a human being and which he puts into motion when he produces useful values.

"But in order to enable the owner of money to meet the labour-power as a commodity in the market, several conditions have to be fulfilled. In itself, the exchange of commodities does not include any other relations of dependence except such as arise from its own nature. On this supposition, labour-power can appear as a commodity, in the market, so far only as it is offered for sale, or sold, by its own owner, the person whose labour-power it is. In order to enable its owner to sell it as a commodity, he must be able to dispose of it, he must be the free proprietor of his labour-power, of his person. He and the owner of money meet in the market, and transact business, as each other's peers, as free and independent owners of commodities, so far different only, that the one is the buyer and the other the seller. This relation of equality before the law must continue; the owner of the labour-power can, therefore, sell it for a limited time only. If he were to sell it in a lump, once for all, he would sell himself, he would from a free man change into a slave, from an owner of a commodity into a commodity.... The second essential condition to enable the money-owner to meet labour-power as a commodity in the market, is this: that the owner of the labour-power, instead of selling commodities in which his labour has been embodied, be compelled to sell this, his labour-power itself, such as it exists in his own personality.

"No producer can sell commodities different from his own labour-power, unless possessed of means of production, raw materials, instruments of labour, etc. He can make no boots without leather. Moreover, he requires the means of subsistence. Nobody can feed upon future products, upon useful values the production of which he has not yet completed; as

32

on the first day of his appearance on the stage of the world, man is compelled to consume before and while he produces. If his products are produced as *commodities*, they must be sold *after* production, and can satisfy his wants after the sale only. The time of production is lengthened·by the time required for sale.

"The change of money into capital, thus, requires that the money-owner meet in the market the *free labourer*, free in that double sense, that he, as a free person, can dispose of his labour-power; and that, on the other hand, he have no other commodities to sell; that he be entirely unencumbered with, perfectly free from, all the things necessary for putting his labour-power into action.

"The question why this free labourer meets him in the market has no interest for the money-owner. For him, the labour-market is only one of the various departments of the general market for commodities. And, for the moment, it has no interest for us either. We stick to the fact theoretically, as he sticks to it practically. One thing, however, is clear. It is not nature which produces, on the one hand, owners of money and of commodities, and on the other, owners of nothing but their own labour-power. This relation does not belong to natural history; nor is it a social relation common to all historical periods. It is evidently the result of a long historical process, the product of a number of economical revolutions, of the destruction of a whole series of older strata of social production.

"The economical categories which we have previously analysed bear in the same manner the impress of their historical origin. The existence of a product in the form of a commodity involves certain historical conditions. In order to become a commodity, the product must not be produced as the immediate means of subsistence of the producer. Now, if we had inquired: How and under what circumstances do all, or at least the great majority of products adopt the form of commodities?—we should have found that this occurs exclusively on the basis of a specific system of production, the *capitalistic* mode of production. But this inquiry was entirely foreign to the analysis of commodity. The production and circulation of commodities may take place, while the overwhelming mass of products—produced for immediate domestic self-use—is never changed into commodities; while, thus, the process of social production, in all its breadth and depth, is, as yet, far from being ruled by value in exchange ...or, in analysing money, we find that the existence of money presupposes a certain development of the circulation of commodities. The peculiar forms of existence of money, such as the form of simple equivalent, or of means of circulation, means of payment, hoard, or universal money, as either one or the other may prevail, point to very different stages of the process of social production. Still, experience shows that a relatively crude state of the circulation of commodities suffices to produce all these forms. But with capital it is quite different. The historical conditions necessary for its existence are far from being created simultaneously with the mere circulation of commodities and money. Capital can originate when the owner of the means of production and subsistence meets, in the market, the free labourer offering for sale his labour-power, and this one condition implies ages of historical development. Thus capital at once heralds itself as a specific epoch of the process of social production." [Pp. 167-70.]

We have now to examine this peculiar commodity, the labour-power. It has a value in exchange, as all other commodities; this value is determined in the same way as that of all other commodities: by the time of labour required for its production, which includes reproduction. The value of labour-power is the value of the means of subsistence necessary for the maintenance of its owner in a normal state of fitness for work. These means of subsistence are regulated by climate and other natural conditions, and by a standard historically established in every country. They vary, but for a given country and a given epoch they are also given. Moreover, they include the means of subsistence for the substitutes of worn-out labourers, for their children, so as to enable this peculiar species of owners of a commodity to perpetuate itself. They include, finally, for skilled labour, the expense of education.

The minimal limit of the value of labour-power is the value of the physically absolute necessaries of life. If its price falls to this limit, it falls below its value, as the latter involves labour-power of normal, not of inferior quality.

The nature of labour makes it evident that labour-power is used *after* the conclusion of the sale only; and in all countries with capitalist mode of production, labour is paid after having been performed. Thus everywhere the labourer gives credit to the capitalist. Of the practical consequences of this credit given by the labourer, Mr. Marx gives some interesting examples from Parliamentary papers, for which we refer to the book itself.

In consuming labour-power, its purchaser produces at once commodities and surplus-value; and in order to examine this, we have to leave the sphere of circulation for that of production.

Here we find at once that the process of labour is of a double nature. On the one hand, it is the simple process of production of useful value; as such, it can and must exist under all historical forms of social existence; on the other hand, it is this process carried on under the specific conditions of capitalistic production, as before stated. These we have now to inquire into.

The process of labour, on a capitalistic basis, has two peculiarities. Firstly, the labourer works under the control of the capitalist who takes care that no waste is made and that no more than the socially indispensable amount of labour is spent upon each individual piece of work. Secondly, the product is the property of the capitalist, the process itself being carried on between two things belonging to him: the labour-power and the means of work.

The capitalist does not care for the useful value, except so far as it is the incorporation of exchangeable value, and above all, of surplus-value. His object is to produce a commodity of a value higher than the sum of value invested in its production. How can this be done?

Let us take a given commodity, say cotton yarn, and analyse the quantity of labour embodied in it. Suppose that for the production of 10 lbs. of yarn we require 10 lbs. of cotton, value 10/- (leaving waste out of consideration). There are further required certain means of work; a steam-engine, carding-engines and other machinery, coal, lubricants, etc. To simplify matters, we call all these "spindle" and suppose that the share of wear and tear, coal, etc., required for spinning 10 lbs. of yarn, is represented by 2/-. Thus we have 10/- cotton + 2/- spindle = 12/-. If 12/- represent the product of 24 working-hours or two working-days, then the cotton and spindle in the yarn incorporate two days' labour. Now, how much is added in the spinning?

We will suppose the value, *per diem*, of labour-power to be 3/-, and these 3/- to represent the labour of six hours. Further, that six hours are required to spin 10 lbs. of yarn by one labourer. In this case 3/- have been added to the product by labour, the value of the 10 lbs. of yarn is 15/- or $\frac{1}{6}$ d. per lb.

This process is very simple, but it does not result in any surplus-value. Nor can it, as in capitalistic production things are not carried on in this simple way.

"We supposed the value of labour-power was 3/- *per diem* and that six hours' labour was represented by that sum.... But if *half*-a-day's labour is required to maintain a labourer for 24 hours, there is nothing in that to prevent the same labourer from working a *whole* day. The exchangeable value of labour-power, and the value which it may produce, are two entirely different quantities, and it was this difference which the capitalist had in his eye when he invested his money in that commodity. That it has the quality of producing useful value, was a more *conditio sine qua non* inasmuch as labour must be invested in a useful form in order to produce value. But our capitalist looked beyond that; what attracted him was the specific circumstance that this labour-power is the source of exchangeable value, and of more exchangeable value than is contained in itself. This is the peculiar 'service' which he expects from it. And in doing so, he acts in accordance with the eternal laws of the exchange of commodities. The seller of the labour-power realises its exchange-value, and parts with its useful value. He cannot obtain the one without giving away the other. The useful value of the labour-power, labour itself, no more belongs to its seller, than the useful value of sold oil to an oil-merchant. The capitalist has paid the value *per diem* of the labour-power; to him, therefore, belongs its use during the day, a day's labour. The circumstance that the maintenance of the labour-power for one day costs half-a-day's labour only, although this labour-power can be made to work a whole day; that, therefore, the value created by its use during a day is twice as great as its own daily value—this circumstance is a peculiar piece of good luck for the buyer, but not at all a wrong inflicted upon the seller."

"The labourer, then, works 12 hours, spins 20 lbs. of yarn representing 20/- in cotton, 4/- in spindle, etc., and his labour costs 3/-,–total 27/-. But if 10 lbs. of cotton absorbed 6 hours of labour, 20 lbs. of cotton have absorbed 12 hours of labour, equal to 6/-. The 20 lbs. of yarn now represent 5 days of labour; 4 in the shape of cotton and spindle, etc., 1 in the shape of spinning labour; the expression, in money, for 5 days' labour, is 30/-; consequently the price of the 20 lbs. of yarn is 30/-, or $1/_6$ d. per lb. as before. But the sum-total of the value of the commodities invested in this process was 27/-. The value of the product has increased beyond the value of the commodities invested in its production by one-ninth. Thus 27/- have been transformed into 30/-. They have produced a surplus-value of 3/-. The trick has, at last, succeeded. Money has been converted into capital.

"All the conditions of the problem have been solved, and the laws of the exchange of commodities have in no way been violated. Equivalent has been exchanged against equivalent. The capitalist, as purchaser, has paid every commodity at its value: cotton, spindles, etc., labour-power. After which, he did what every buyer of commodities does. He consumed their useful value. The process of consumption of the labour-power, at the same time a process of production of the commodity, resulted in a product of 20 lbs. of yarn, value 30/-. Our capitalist returns to the market and sells the yarn at $1/_6$ d. per lb., not a fraction above or below its value, and yet he extracts 3/- more from circulation than he originally invested in it. The whole of this process, the transformation of his money into capital, passes within the sphere of circulation, and at the same time *not* within it. By the intervention of circulation, because the purchase, in the market, of the labour-power was its indispensable condition. Not within the sphere of circulation, because this merely initiates the process of value begetting value, which is performed in the sphere of production. And thus *tout est pour le mieux dans le meilleur des mondes possibles.*" [Pp. 190, 193-95.]

From the demonstration of the mode in which surplus-value is produced, Mr. Marx passes to its analysis. It is evident, from what precedes, that only one portion of the capital invested in any productive undertaking directly contributes to the production of surplus-value, and that is the capital laid out in the purchase of labour-power. This portion only produces *new* value; the capital invested in machinery, raw materials, coal, etc., does indeed re-appear in the value of the product *pro tanto*, it is maintained and reproduced, but no surplus-value can proceed from it. This induces Mr. Marx to propose a new subdivision of capital into *constant* capital, that which is merely reproduced—the portion invested in machinery, raw materials and all other accessories to labour; —and *variable* capital, that which is not only reproduced, but is, at the same time, the direct source of surplus-value— that portion which is invested in the purchase of labour-power, in wages. From this it is clear, that however necessary constant capital may be to the production of surplus-value, yet it does not directly contribute to it; and, moreover, the amount of constant capital invested in any trade has not the slightest influence upon the amount of surplus-value produced in that trade.[1] Consequently, it ought not to be taken into consideration in fixing the *rate* of surplus-value. That can be determined only by comparing the amount of surplus-value to the amount of capital directly engaged in creating it, that is to say, the amount of *variable* capital. Mr. Marx, therefore, determines the rate of surplus-value by its proportion to variable capital only: if the daily price of labour be 3/-, and the surplus-value created daily be also 3/-, then he calls the rate of surplus-value 100 per cent. What curious blunders may result from reckoning, according to usual practice, constant capital as an active factor in the production of surplus-value, is shown in an example from Mr. N. W. Senior "when that Oxford professor, noted for his scientific attainments and his beautiful diction, was invited, in 1836, to Manchester, in order to learn political economy there (from the cotton spinners) instead of teaching it in Oxford". [P. 224.]

The working-time in which the labourer reproduces the value of his labour-power, Mr. Marx calls *"necessary labour"*; the time worked beyond that, and during which surplus-value is produced, he calls *"surplus-labour"*. Necessary labour and surplus-labour combined form the *"working-day"*.

In a working-day the time required for necessary labour is given; but the time employed in surplus-labour is not fixed by any economical law, it may be longer or shorter, within

---

[1] We must observe, here, that *surplus-value* is not at all identical with *profit*.

certain limits. It can never be zero, as then the inducement for the capitalist to employ labour would have ceased; nor can the total length of the working-day ever attain 24 hours, for physiological reasons. Between a working-day of, say, six hours, and one of 24, there are, however, many intermediate stages. The laws of the exchange of commodities demand that the working-day have a length not exceeding that which is compatible with the normal wear and tear of the labourer. But what is this normal wear and tear? How many hours of daily labour are compatible with it? Here the opinions of the capitalist and those of the labourer differ widely, and, as there is no higher authority, the question is solved by *force*. The history of the determination of the length of the working-day is the history of a struggle about its limits between the collective capitalist and the collective labourer, between the two classes of capitalists and workingmen.

"Capital, as has been stated before, has not invented surplus-labour. Wherever a portion of society holds the exclusive monopoly of the means of production, there the labourer, slave, serf, or free, has to add, to the labour necessary for his own subsistence, an increment of labour in order to produce the means of subsistence for the owner of the means of production, be that owner an Athenian χαλός χἀγαθός[1], an Etruscan theocrat, a *civis Romanus*, a Norman baron, an American slave-owner, a Wallachian boyar, a modern landlord or capitalist." [P. 235.] It is, however, evident that in any form of society where the value in use of the product is more important than its value in exchange, surplus-labour is restrained by the narrower or wider range of social wants; and that under these circumstances there does not exist necessarily a desire for surplus-labour for its own sake. Thus we find that in the classical period surplus-labour in its extremist form, the working to death of people, existed almost exclusively in gold and silver mines, where value in exchange was produced in its independent form of existence: money. But wherever a nation whose production is carried on in the more rudimentary forms of slavery or serfage, lives in the midst of a universal market dominated by capitalist production, and

---

[1] Aristocrat. – *Ed.*

where therefore the sale of its products for exports forms its chief purpose—there to the barbarous infamies of slavery or serfdom are superadded the civilised infamies of overworking. Thus in the Southern States of America slave-labour preserved a moderate and patriarchal character while production was directed to immediate domestic consumption chiefly. But in the same measure as the export of cotton became a vital interest to those states, the overworking of the Negro, in some instances even the wearing-out of his life in seven working years, became an element in a calculated and calculating system.... Similar with the *corvée* of the serfs in the Danubian principalities." [Pp. 235-36.] Here the comparison with capitalist production becomes particularly interesting, because, in the *corvée*, surplus-labour has an independent, palpable form.

"Suppose the working-day counts six hours of necessary and six hours of surplus-labour; then the labourer furnishes the capitalist with 36 hours of surplus-labour a week. He might as well have worked three days for himself and three days for the capitalist. But this is not at once visible. Surplus-labour and necessary labour are more or less mixed together. I might express the same relation thus, that, in every minute, the labourer works 30 seconds for himself and 30 more for the capitalist. But with the serfs' *corvée* it is different. The two kinds of labour are separated in space. The labour, which, for instance, a Wallachian peasant performs for himself, he performs on his own field, his surplus-labour for the boyar he performs on the boyar's estate. The two portions of his labour exist independent of each other, surplus-labour, in the shape of *corvée*, is completely separated from necessary labour." [P. 236.] We must refrain from quoting the further interesting illustrations from the modern social history of the Danubian principalities, by which Mr. Marx proves the boyars there, aided by Russian intervention, to be quite as clever extractors of surplus-labour as any capitalist employers. But what the *règlement organique*, by which the Russian General Kisseleff presented the boyars with almost unlimited command over the peasants' labour, expresses positively, the English Factory Acts express negatively. "These acts oppose the inherent tendency of capital to an unlimited exploitation—we ask pardon for introducing this French term, but there does not exist any English

40

equivalent—of the labour-power, by forcibly putting a limit to the length of the working-day by the power of the State, and that a State ruled by landlords and capitalists. Not to speak of the working-class movement which was daily gaining greater dimensions, this limitation of factory labour was dictated by the same necessity which brought Peruvian guano on the fields of England. The same blind rapacity which in the one case had exhausted the soil, in the other case had attacked the vitality of the nation at its root. Periodical epidemics here spoke as plainly, as, in France and Germany, the necessity for constantly reducing the standard of height for soldiers." [P. 239.]

To prove the tendency of capital to extend the working-day beyond all reasonable limits Mr. Marx quotes amply from the Reports of the Factory Inspectors, of the Children's Employment Commission, the Reports on Public Health and other Parliamentary Papers, and sums up in the following conclusions:

"What is a working-day? How long is the time during which capital may be allowed to consume the working power on paying for its value *per diem*? How far may the working-day be extended beyond the time necessary for reproducing the working power itself? Capital, as we have seen, replies: the working-day counts full 24 hours, excepting those few hours of rest without which the labour-power absolutely refuses to renew its services. It is a matter of course that the labourer during the whole of the live-long day is nothing but labour-power, that all his disposable time is working-time and belongs to value-begetting capital.... But in this madly blind race after surplus-labour, capital outruns not only the moral, but also the purely physical maximum limits of the working-day.... Capital does not care for the duration of life of the working power ... it produces its premature exhaustion and death, it effects the prolongation of the working-time during a given period by shortening the labourer's life." [Pp. 264-65.]

But is not this against the interests of capital itself? Has capital, in the long run, not to replace the cost of this excessive wear and tear? That may be the case theoretically. Practically, the organised slave trade in the interior of the Southern States had raised the practice of using up the working power of the slave in seven years to an acknowledged economical principle; practically, the English capitalist relies upon the supply of labourers from the agricultural districts. "He sees a constant over-population, that is, an over-population as compared with the capacity of capital to absorb living labour, though this over-population be formed by a constant current of crippled, quickly fading generations of men, pressing upon their successors and plucked before maturity. Certainly, to an uninterested observer, experience would show on the other hand how soon capitalist production, though dating, historically speaking, from yesterday only, has attacked the vital root of national strength, how the degeneration of the industrial population is retarded only by the constant absorption of agricultural elements, and how even these agricultural labourers, in spite of fresh air and that principle of natural selection which is so specially powerful amongst them, have already begun to decline. Capital, which has such capital motives to deny the sufferings of the working classes in the midst of which it exists, capital will be disturbed in its practical activity as little and as much by the prospect of future degeneracy of the human race and of inevitable ultimate depopulation, as by the possible fall of the earth into the sun. In every joint-stock 'limited' swindle, every participator knows that the thunderstorm will come sooner or later, but every one expects that the lightning will fall on the head of his neighbour, after he himself shall have had time to collect the golden rain and store it up safely. *Après moi le déluge* is the battle-cry of every capitalist and of every capitalist nation. Capital, therefore, is reckless of the health and life of the labourer, unless society compels it to act otherwise. And, upon the whole, this disregard of the labourer does not depend upon the good or bad will of the individual capitalist. Free competition imposes the immanent laws of capitalist production upon every individual capitalist in the shape of extraneous compulsory laws." [Pp. 269-70.]

The determination of the normal working-day is the result of many centuries of struggle between employer and labourer. And it is curious to observe the two opposing currents in this struggle. At first, the laws have for their end to compel the labourers to work longer hours; from the first statute of labourers (23rd Edward III, 1349) up to the eighteenth century, the ruling classes never succeeded in extorting from the labourer the full amount of possible labour. But with the introduction of steam and modern machinery, the tables were turned. So rapidly did the introduction of the labour of women and children break down all traditional bounds to working-hours, that the nineteenth century began with a system of overworking which is unparalleled in the history of the world, and which, as early as 1803, compelled the legislature to enact limitations of working-hours. Mr. Marx gives a full account of the history of English factory legislation up to the Workshops Act of 1867, and draws from it these conclusions:

1) Machinery and steam cause overwork, at first, in those branches of industry where they are applied, and legislative restrictions are, therefore, first applied to these branches; but in the sequel we find that this system of overwork has spread also to almost all trades, even where no machinery is used, or where the most primitive modes of production continue in existence. (*Vide* Children's Employment Commission's Reports.)

2) With the introduction of the labour of women and children in the factories, the individual "free" labourer loses his power of resistance to the encroachments of capital and has to submit unconditionally. Thus he is reduced to collective resistance; the struggle of class against class, of the collective workmen against the collective capitalists begins.

If we now look back to the moment when we supposed our "free" and "equal" labourer to enter into a contract with the capitalist, we find that, under the process of production, a good many things have changed considerably. That contract, on the part of the labourer, is not a free contract. The daily time during which he is at liberty to sell his working power is the time during which he is compelled to sell it; and it is merely the opposition of the labourers, as a mass, which forcibly obtains the enactment of a public law to prevent them from selling themselves and their children, by a "free" contract, into death and slavery. "In the place of the grandiloquent catalogue of the inalienable rights of man, he has now nothing but the modest *Magna Charta* of the Factory Act." [P. 302.]

We have next to analyse the *rate* of surplus-value and its relation to the *total quantity* of surplus-value produced. In this inquiry, as we have done hitherto, we suppose the value of labour-power to be a determinate constant quantity.

Under this supposition, the rate of surplus-value determines at the same time the quantity furnished to the capitalist by a single labourer in a given time. If the value of our labour-power be 3/- a day, representing six hours' labour, and the rate of surplus-value be 100 per cent, then the variable capital of 3/- produces every day a surplus-value of 3/-, or the workman furnishes six hours of surplus-labour every day.

Variable capital being the expression in money of all the labour-power employed simultaneously by a capitalist, the sum-total of the surplus-value produced by the labour-power is found by multiplying that variable capital by the rate of surplus-value; in other words it is determined by the proportion between the number of working powers simultaneously employed, and the degree of exploitation. Either of these factors may vary, so that the decrease in the one may be compensated by the increase in the other. A variable capital required to employ 100 labourers with a rate of surplus-value of 50 per cent (say three hours of daily surplus-labour) will produce no more surplus-value than half that variable capital, employing 50 labourers at a rate of surplus-value of 100 per cent (say six hours of daily surplus-labour). Thus, under certain circumstances and within certain limits, the supply of labour at the command of capital may become independent of the actual supply of labourers.

There is, however, an absolute limit to this increase of surplus-value by increasing its rate. Whatever may be the value of labour, whether it be represented by two or by ten hours of necessary labour, the total value of the work performed, day after day, by any labourer, can never attain the value representing 24 hours' labour. In order to obtain equal quantities of surplus-value, variable capital may be replaced by prolongation of the working-day within this limit only. This will be an important element in explaining, hereafter, various phenomena arising from the two contradictory tendencies of capital: 1) to reduce the number of labourers employed, i.e., the amount of variable capital, and 2) yet to produce the greatest possible quantity of surplus-labour.

It follows further: "The value of labour being given, and the rate of surplus-value being equal, the quantities of surplus-value produced by two different capitals are in direct proportion to the quantities of variable capital contained in them. ... This law flatly contradicts all experience founded upon the *appearance* of facts. Everybody knows that a cotton spinner who works with a relatively large constant, and a relatively small variable capital, does not, on that account, obtain a lesser ratio of profit· than a baker who puts in motion relatively little constant and relatively much variable capital. To solve this apparent contradiction, a good many intermediate links are required, just as, starting from elementary algebra, a great number of intermediate links are required in order to understand that 0 : 0 may represent a real quantity." [P. 307.]

For a given country and a given length of working-day, surplus-value can be increased only by increasing the number of labourers, *i.e.*, by an increase of population; this increase forms the mathematical limit for the production of surplus-value by the collective capital of that country. On the other hand, if the number of labourers be determined, this limit is fixed by the possible prolongation of the working-day. It will be seen hereafter that this law is valid only for that form of surplus-value which has been hitherto analysed.

We find, at this stage of our inquiry, that not every amount of money is capable of being converted into capital; that there is an extreme minimum for it: the cost of a unit of labouring power and of the means of labour necessary to keep it going. Suppose the rate of surplus-value to be 50 per cent, our infant capitalist would be required to be able to employ two workmen in order to live, himself, as a workman lives. But this would prevent him from saving anything; and the end of capitalist production is not merely preservation, but also and chiefly increase of wealth. "To live twice as well as a common labourer, and to re-transform one-half of the surplus-value produced into capital, he would have to be able to employ eight workmen. He might certainly take his share of the work, along with his workmen, but he would still remain a small master, a hybrid between capitalist and labourer. Now, a certain development of capitalist production renders it necessary that the capitalist should devote the whole of the time, during which he acts as a capitalist, as capital personified, to the appropriation and control of other people's labour, and to the sale of its products. The restrictive guilds of the Middle Ages attempted to check the transformation of the small master into a capitalist by fixing a very low maximum to the number of workmen which each was allowed to employ. The owner of money or commodities changes into a real capitalist only then, when he is able to advance for the purpose of production, a minimum sum far higher than this medieval maximum. Here, just as in the natural sciences, the correctness is proved of the law discovered by Hegel that mere quantitative changes, at a certain point, imply a qualitative difference." [Pp. 308-09.] The minimum amount of value required to change an owner of money or commodities into a capitalist varies for different stages of the development of capitalist production, and for a given stage of development, it varies for different branches of industry.

During the process of production detailed above, the relation of capitalist and labourer has changed considerably. "First of all, capital has been developed into command of labour, *i.e.*, into command over the labourer himself. Personified capital, the capitalist, takes care that the labourer performs his work regularly, carefully and with the required degree of intensity. Further, capital has been developed into a. compulsory relation which obliges the working class to perform more labour than is prescribed by the narrow circle of their own requirements. And as a producer of other people's industry, as an extortioner of surplus-labour and exploiter of labour-power, capital far exceeds in energy, recklessness, and efficiency all former systems of production, though they were based upon direct forced labour.

"Capital, at first, takes the command of labour under such technological conditions as it finds historically established. It does not, therefore, necessarily at once change the mode of production. The production of surplus-value, in the form hitherto analysed, that is to say by mere prolongation of the working-day, appeared independent of every change in the mode of production itself. It was quite as efficient in the primitive baking trade as in modern cotton-spinning.

"In the process of production considered as a mere process of labour, the relation between the labourer and his means of production is not that of labour and capital, but that of labour and the mere instrument and raw material of productive action. In a tannery, for instance, he treats the skins as a mere object for labour. It is not the capitalist whose skin he tans. But things change as soon as we look upon the process of production as a process of creating surplus-value. The means of production at once change into means of absorbing other people's labour. It is no longer the workman who employs the means of production, it is the means of production which employ the workman. It is not he who consumes *them* as material elements of his productive action; it is they which consume *him* as the ferment of their own vital process; and the vital process of capital consists in nothing but its progressive motion as value begetting value. Furnaces and workshops which have to stand idle at night, without absorbing labour, are a pure loss to the capitalist. Therefore furnaces and workshops constitute a title upon the night-work of the hands'. (See Reports of Children's Empl. Commission, 4th Report, 1865, pages 79 to 85.) The mere change of money into means of production changes the latter into legal and compulsory titles upon other people's labour and surplus-labour." [Pp. 309-10.]

There is, however, another form of surplus-value. Arrived at the utmost limit of the working-day, another means remains to the capitalist for increasing surplus-labour: by increasing the productivity of labour, by thereby reducing the value of labour, and thus shortening the period of necessary labour. This form of surplus-value will be examined in a second article.

SAMUEL MOORE.[1]

---

[1] To facilitate publication in England, Engels's friend Moore signed this review.—*Ed.*

II

SYNOPSIS OF *CAPITAL*

K. MARX. *CAPITAL*

Volume One. Book One

THE PROCESS
OF CAPITALIST PRODUCTION

*Translated from a photocopy
in the possession of the Institute
of Marxism-Leninism*

CHAPTER I

COMMODITIES AND MONEY

1. COMMODITIES AS SUCH

The wealth of societies in which capitalist production prevails consists of *commodities.* A commodity is a thing that has *use-value;* the latter exists in all forms of society, but in capitalist society, use-value is, in addition, the material depository of *exchange-value.*

Exchange-value presupposes a *tertium comparationis* by which it is measured: labour, the common social substance of exchange-values, to be precise, the *socially necessary labour-time* embodied in them.

Just as a commodity is something twofold: use-value and exchange-value, so the labour contained in it is twofold determined: on the one hand, as *definite productive activity,* weaving labour, tailoring labour, etc.—*"useful labour";* on the other, as the *simple expenditure of human labour-power, precipitated abstract (general) labour.* The former produces use-value, the latter exchange-value; only the latter is quantitatively comparable (the differences between skilled and unskilled, composite and simple labour *confirm* this).

Hence the substance of exchange-value is abstract labour and its magnitude is the measure of time of abstract labour. Now to consider the form of exchange-value.

(1) x commodity $a = y$ commodity $b;$ the value of a commodity in the use-value of another is its *relative value.* The expression of the equivalence of two commodities is the simple form of relative value. In the above equation y *commodity b* is the *equivalent.* In it x *commodity a* acquires its value-form in contrast to its (the commodity's) natural form,

while y *commodity* b acquires at the same time the property of direct exchangeability, even in its natural form. Exchange-value is impressed upon the use-value of a commodity by definite historical relations. Hence the commodity cannot express its exchange-value in its own use-value, but only in the use-value of another commodity. Only in the equation of two concrete products of labour does the property of the concrete labour contained in both come to light as abstract human labour, *i.e.*, a commodity cannot be related to the concrete labour contained in itself, as the mere form of realisation of abstract labour, but it can be so related to the concrete labour contained in other kinds of commodities.

The equation x commodity $a = y$ commodity b necessarily implies that x commodity a can also be expressed in other commodities, thus:

(2) x commodity $a = y$ commodity $b = z$ commodity $c = v$ commodity $d = u$ commodity $e =$, etc., etc. This is the *expanded* relative form of value. Here x commodity a no longer refers to one, but to all commodities as the mere phenomenal forms of the labour represented in it. But through simple reversal it leads to

(3) the converse second form of relative value:

$$y \text{ commodity } b = x \text{ commodity } a$$
$$v \text{ commodity } c = x \text{ commodity } a$$
$$u \text{ commodity } d = x \text{ commodity } a$$
$$t \text{ commodity } e = x \text{ commodity } a$$

etc., etc.

Here the commodities are given the *general relative form of value*, in which all of them are abstracted from their use-values and equated to x commodity a as the materialisation of abstract labour; x commodity a is the generic form of the equivalent for all other commodities; it is their *universal equivalent*; the labour materialised in it represents in itself the realisation of abstract labour, labour in general. Now, however,

(4) *every* commodity of the series can take over the role of universal equivalent, but only one of them can do so *at a time*, since if *all* commodities were universal equivalents, each of them would in turn exclude the others from that role. Form 3 is not obtained by x commodity *a*, but by the other commodities, objectively. Hence a definite commodity must

take over the role—for a time, it can change—and only in this way does a commodity become a commodity completely. This special commodity, with whose natural form the general equivalent form becomes identified, is *money*.

The difficulty with a *commodity* is that, like all categories of the capitalist mode of production, it represents a personal relationship under a material wrapping. The producers relate their different kinds of labour to one another as general human labour by relating their products to one another as *commodities*—they cannot accomplish it without this mediation of things. The relation of *persons* thus *appears* as the relation of *things*.

For a society in which commodity production prevails, Christianity, particularly Protestantism, is the fitting religion.

2. THE PROCESS OF COMMODITY EXCHANGE

A commodity proves that it is a commodity in exchange. The owners of two commodities must be willing to exchange their respective commodities and therefore to recognise each other as *private owners*. This legal relation, the *form* of which is the contract, is only a relation of wills, reflecting the economic relation. Its *content* is given by the economic relation itself. (P. 45 [84].)

A commodity is a use-value for its non-owner, a non-use-value for its owner. Hence the need for exchange. But every commodity owner wants to get in exchange specific use-values that he needs—to that extent the exchange is an individual process. On the other hand, he wants to realise his commodity as value, that is, in any commodity, whether or not *his* commodity is use-value to the owner of the other commodity. To that extent the exchange is for him a generally social process. But one and the same process cannot be simultaneously both individual and generally social for all commodity owners. Every commodity owner considers *his own* commodity as the universal equivalent, while all other commodities are so many particular equivalents of his own. Since *all* commodity owners do the same, *no* commodity is the universal equivalent, and hence *no* commodities possess a general relative form of value, in which they are equated as values and compared as magnitudes of value. Therefore they do not confront each other at all as commodities, but only as products. (P. 47 [86].)

Commodities can be related as values and hence as commodities only by comparison with some other commodity as the universal equivalent. But only the *social act can make a particular commodity the universal equivalent—money.*

The immanent contradiction in a commodity as the direct unity of use-value and exchange-value, as the product of useful private labour... and as the direct social materialisation of abstract human labour—this contradiction finds no rest until it results in duplicating the commodity into commodity and money. (P. 48[87].)

Since all other commodities are merely particular equivalents of money, and money is their universal equivalent, they are related to money as *particular* commodities to the universal commodity. (P. 51 [89].) The process of exchange gives the commodity which it converts into money, not its *value*, but its *value-form* (P. 51 [90].) Fetishism (belief in a supernatural power of objects): a commodity does not seem to become money only because the other commodities all express their values in it, but·conversely, they seem to express their values in it because it *is money.*

3. MONEY, OR THE CIRCULATION OF COMMODITIES

A. The Measure of Values
(Assuming Gold = Money)

Money, as the measure of value, is the necessary *phenomenal form* of the measure of value *immanent* in commodities, *i.e., labour-time.* The simple, relative expression of the value of commodities in money, x commodity $a = y$ money, is their price. (P. 55 [95].)

The price of a commodity, its money-form, is expressed in *imaginary* money; hence money is the *measure of values* only ideally. (P. 57 [95].)

Once the change from value to price is effected, it becomes technically necessary to develop the measure of values further, into the *standard of price; i.e.,* a quantity of gold is fixed, *by which different quantities of gold are measured.* This is quite different from the measure of values, which itself depends upon the value of gold, while the latter is immaterial for the standard of prices. (P. 59[97-98].)

Once prices are expressed in accounting names of gold, money serves as *money of account.*

If price, as the exponent of the magnitude of a commodity's value, is the exponent of its exchange ratio with money it does *not* follow conversely that the exponent of its exchange ratio with money is *necessarily* the exponent of the magnitude of its value. Assuming that circumstances permit or compel the sale of a commodity above or below its value, these selling prices do not correspond to its value, but they are none the less *prices* of the commodity, for they are (1) its value-form, money, and (2) exponents of its exchange ratio with money.

The possibility, therefore, of quantitative incongruity between price and magnitude of value is *given in the price-form itself.* That is no defect of this form, but on the contrary makes it the adequate form of a mode of production in which the rule can impose itself only as a blindly-acting law of averages of irregularity. The price-form, however, can also harbour a qualitative contradiction, so that price ceases altogether to be an expression of value.... Conscience, honour, etc., can ... acquire the form of commodities through their price. (P. 61 [102].)

Measurement of values in money, the price-form, implies the necessity of alienation, the ideal pricing implies the actual. Hence circulation.

B. *The Medium of Circulation*

a. The Metamorphosis of Commodities

Simple form: *C–M–C.* Its material content=*C–C.* Exchange-value is alienated and use-value appropriated.

α First phase: *C–M*=sale, for which two persons are required, hence the possibility of failure, *i.e.,* of sale below value, or even below the cost of production, if the social value of the commodity changes. "The division of labour converts the product of labour into a commodity, and thereby makes *necessary* its further conversion into money." At the same time it also makes the accomplishment of this transubstantiation quite accidental. (P. 67[108].) But, considering the phenomenon in its *pure* form, *C–M* presupposes that the possessor of the money (unless he is a producer of gold) previously got his money through exchange for other commodities; hence it is not only conversely *M–C* for the *buyer*, but it presupposes that he made a previous sale, etc., so that we have an endless series of purchases and sales.

β The same takes place in the second phase, *M–C*, *i.e., purchase*, which is, at the same time, a sale for the other party.

γ The total process hence is a circuit of purchases and sales. *The circulation of commodities*. This is quite different from the direct exchange of products; first, the individual and local bounds of the direct exchange of products are broken through, and the metabolism of human labour is made possible; on the other hand, here it already appears that the whole process depends upon social relations spontaneous in their growth and independent of the actors. (P. 72 [112].) Simple exchange was extinguished in the one act of exchange, where each exchanges non-use-value for use-value; circulation proceeds indefinitely. (P. 73 [112].)

Here the false economic dogma: *the circulation of commodities involves a necessary equilibrium of purchases and sales, because every purchase is also a sale and vice versa–which is to say that every seller also brings his buyer to market with him*. (1) Purchase and sale are, on the one hand, an identical act of two polarly opposite persons (poles are the two ends of the axis of a sphere); on the other hand, they are two polarly opposite acts of one and the same person. Hence the identity of purchase and sale implies that the commodity is useless unless it is sold, and likewise that this case *can* occur. (2) *C–M*, as a partial process, is similarly an independent process and implies that the acquirer of money can choose the time when he again converts this money into a commodity. He can *wait*. The inner unity of the independent processes *C–M* and *M–C* moves in external antitheses precisely because of the independence of these processes; and when these dependent processes reach a certain limit of independence, *their unity asserts itself in a c r i s i s*. Hence the *possibility* of the latter is already given here.

Being the intermediary in commodity circulation, money is the *medium of circulation*.

b. The Currency of Money

Money is the medium by which each individual commodity goes into, and out of, circulation; it always remains therein itself. Hence, although the circulation of money is merely the *expression* of commodity circulation, the circulation of commodities *appears* to be the result of money circulation. Since money always remains within the sphere of circulation, the question is: *how much* money is present in it?

The quantity of money in circulation is determined by the *sum of the prices of commodities* (money-value remaining the same), and the latter by the *quantity of commodities* in circulation. Assuming that this quantity of commodities is given, the circulating quantity of money fluctuates with the *fluctuations* in the prices of commodities. Now, since one and the same coin always mediates a number of transactions in succession in a given time, for a given interval of time we have:

$$\frac{\text{Sum of the prices of commodities}}{\text{Number of moves made by a piece of money}} = \begin{array}{c}\text{Quantity of money functioning} \\ \text{as the circulating medium.} \\ \text{(P. 80 [120].)}\end{array}$$

Hence paper money can displace gold money if it is thrown into a saturated circulation.

Since the currency of money only *reflects* the process of commodity circulation, its rapidity reflects that of the change in the form of the commodities, its stagnation, the separation of purchase from sale, the stagnation of social metabolism. The origin of this stagnation cannot, of course, be seen from circulation itself, which puts in evidence only the phenomenon. The philistines attribute it to a deficient quantity of the circulating medium. (P. 81 [121].)

Ergo: (1) If the prices of commodities remain constant, the quantity of money circulating rises when the quantity of circulating commodities increases or the circulation of money is retarded; and drops *vice versa.*

(2) With a general rise in the prices of commodities, the quantity of money circulating remains constant if the quantity of commodities decreases or the velocity of circulation increases in the same proportion.

(3) With a general drop in the prices of commodities, the converse of (2).

In general, there is a fairly constant average from which appreciable deviations occur almost exclusively as a result of *crises*.

c. Coin. Symbols of Value

The standard of prices is fixed by the state, as are also the denomination of the particular piece of gold—the coin, and its coining. In the world market the respective national uniforms are doffed again (seigniorage is disregarded here), so that coin and bullion differ only in form. But *a coin wears away* during circulation; gold as a circulating medium differs from gold as a standard of prices. The coin becomes more and more a *symbol* of its official content.

Herewith the latent possibility is given of replacing metallic money by tokens or symbols. Hence: (1) small coinage of copper and silver tokens, the permanent establishment of which in place of real gold money is prevented by limiting the quantity in which they are legal tender. Their metallic content is determined purely arbitrarily by law, and thus their function as coinage becomes independent of their *value*. Hence the further step to *quite worthless* symbols is possible: (2) paper money, *i.e.*, *paper money issued by the state, having compulsory circulation*. (Credit money not to be discussed here as yet.) So far as this paper money actually circulates in place of gold money, it is subject to the laws of money circulation. Only the proportion in which paper replaces gold can be the object of a special law, which is: that the issue of paper money is to be limited to the quantity in which the gold represented by it would actually have to circulate. The degree of saturation of circulation fluctuates, but everywhere experience determines a minimum below which it never falls. This minimum can be issued. If more than the minimum is issued, a portion becomes superfluous as soon as the degree of saturation drops to the minimum. In that case the total amount of paper money within the commodity world still represents only the quantity of gold fixed by that world's immanent laws, and hence alone representable. Thus, if the amount of paper money represents twice the absorbable amount of gold, each piece of paper money is depreciated to half its nominal value. Just as if gold were changed in its function as the measure of prices, in its value. (P. 89 [128].)

C. Money

a. Hoarding

With the earliest development of commodity circulation there develops the need, and the passionate desire, to hold fast the product of *C–M*, money. From a mere agency of change of matter, this change of form becomes an *end in itself*. Money petrifies into a *hoard*; the commodity seller becomes a money *hoarder*. (P. 91 [130].)

This form was dominant precisely in the beginnings of commodity circulation. *Asia*. With further development of commodity circulation every producer of commodities must secure for himself the *nexus rerum*, the social pledge—money. Thus hoards accumulate everywhere. The development of commodity circulation increases the power of money, the absolutely social form of wealth, always ready for use. (P. 92 [131].) The urge for hoarding is by nature boundless. *Qualitatively*, or with respect to its form, money is unrestricted, *i.e.*, the universal representative of material wealth, because it is directly convertible into any commodity. But *quantitatively*, every actual sum of money is limited, and therefore of only limited efficacy as a means of purchasing. This contradiction always drives the hoarder back, again and again, to the Sisyphus-like (vain) labour of accumulation.

Besides, the accumulation of gold and silver in plate creates both a new market for these metals and a latent source of money.

Hoarding serves as a *conduit for supplying or withdrawing circulating money* with the continuous fluctuations in the degree of saturation of the circulation. (P. 95 [134].)

b. Means of Payment

With the development of commodity circulation new conditions appear: the alienation of a commodity can be separated in time from the realisation of its price. Commodities require

59

different periods of time for their production; they are produced in different seasons; some must be sent to distant markets, etc. Hence *A* can be a seller before *B*, the buyer, is able to pay. Practice regulates the conditions of payment in this way: *A* becomes a *creditor*, *B* a *debtor*; money becomes a *means of payment*. Thus the relation of *creditor* and *debtor* already becomes *more antagonistic*. (This can also occur independently of commodity circulation, *e.g.*, in antiquity and the Middle Ages.) (P. 97 [135].)

In this relation, money functions: (1) as the measure of value in the determination of the price of the commodity sold; (2) as an ideal means of purchase. In the hoard, money was *withdrawn* from circulation; here, being a means of payment, money enters circulation, but only after the commodity has left it. The indebted buyer sells in order to be able *to pay*, or he will be put up for auction. Therefore, money now becomes *the sale's end in itself* through a social necessity arising out of the relations of the very circulation process. (Pp. 97-98 [136].)

The lack of simultaneity of purchases and sales, which gives rise to the function of money as a means of payment, at the same time effects an economy of the circulation media, payments being concentrated at a definite place. The *virements* (remittance by draft from own account to another) in Lyons in the Middle Ages—a sort of clearing-house, where only the net balance of the mutual claims is paid. (P. 98 [137].)

In so far as the payments balance one another, money functions only ideally, as *money of account* or measure of values. In so far as actual payment has to be made, it does not appear as a circulating medium, as only the vanishing and mediating form of metabolism, but as the individual embodiment of social labour, as the independent existence of exchange-value, as the *absolute commodity*. This *direct contradiction* breaks out in that phase of production and commercial crises that is called *a monetary crisis*. It occurs only where the progressing chain of payments, and an artificial system of settling them, are fully developed. With more general disturbances of this mechanism, no matter what their origin, money changes suddenly and immediately from its merely ideal shape of *money of account into hard cash*; profane commodities can no longer replace it. (P. 99 [138].)

Credit money originates in the function of money as a means of payment; certificates of debt themselves circulate in turn to transfer these debts to others. With the system of credit the function of money as a means of payment again expands; in that capacity money acquires its own forms of existence, in which it occupies the sphere of large-scale commercial transactions, while coin is largely relegated to the sphere of retail trade. (P. 101 [139-40].)

At a certain stage and volume of commodity production the function of money as a means of payment spreads beyond the sphere of the circulation of commodities; it becomes the *universal commodity of contracts. Rents, taxes,* and the like are transformed from *payments in kind* into *money payments.* Cf. France under Louis XIV. (Boisguillebert and Vauban); on the other hand, Asia, Turkey, Japan, etc. (P. 102 [140-41].)

The·development of money into a means of payment necessitates the accumulation of money against the date when payment is due. Hoarding which, as a distinct form of acquiring riches, vanished as society further developed, again appears as a reserve fund of the means of payment. (P. 103 [142].)

c. Universal Money

In world trade the local forms of coin, small coinage, and paper money are discarded and only the bullion form of money is valid as *universal money. Only in the world market does money function to the full extent as the commodity whose bodily form is at the same time the immediate social incarnation of human labour in the abstract.* Its mode of existence becomes adequate to its concept. (Pp. 103-04 [142]; details p. 105 [145].)

CHAPTER II

THE TRANSFORMATION OF MONEY
INTO CAPITAL

1. THE GENERAL FORMULA
FOR CAPITAL

The circulation of commodities is the starting point of capital. Hence commodity production, commodity circulation and the latter's developed form, commerce, are always the historical groundwork from which capital arises. The modern history of capital dates from the creation of modern world trade and the world market in the sixteenth century. (P. 106 [146].)

If we consider only the economic forms produced by commodity circulation, we find that its final product is money, and the latter is the *first form in which capital appears.* Historically, capital invariably confronts landed property at first as *moneyed wealth,* the capital of the merchant and the usurer, and even today all new capital first comes on the stage in the shape of *money* that by definite processes has to be transformed into capital.

Money as money and money as capital differ, to begin with, only in their *form of circulation.* Alongside *C–M–C,* the form *M–C–M,* buying in order to sell, also occurs. Money that describes *this* form of circulation in its movement *becomes* capital, is already capital in itself *(i.e.,* by its destination).

The result of *M–C–M* is *M–M,* the indirect exchange of money for money. I buy cotton for £100 and sell it for £110; ultimately I have exchanged £100 for £110, money for money.

If this process yielded at its outcome the same money-value that was originally put into it, £100 out of £100, it would be absurd. Yet whether the merchant realises £100, £110, or merely £50 for his £100, his money has described a specific movement quite different from that of commodity circulation, *C–M–C.* From the examination of the differences in form between this movement and *C–M–C* the difference in content will also be found.

The two phases of the process taken separately are the same as in *C–M–C.* But there is a great difference in the process as a whole. In *C–M–C* money constitutes the intermediary, the commodity the starting point and the finish; in this case the commodity is the intermediary, with money the starting point and the finish. In *C–M–C* the money is spent once for all; in *M–C–M* it is merely *advanced,* it is to be got back again. *It flows back to its starting point.* Here, therefore, is already a palpable difference between the circulation of money as money and money as capital.

In *C–M–C* money can return to its starting point only through the *repetition of the whole process,* through the sale of *fresh* commodities. Hence the reflux is independent of the process itself. In *M–C–M*, on the other hand, it is conditioned from the outset by the structure of the process itself, which is incomplete if the return flow fails. (P. 110 [149].)

The ultimate object of *C–M–C* is use-value, that of *M–C–M exchange-value itself.*

In *C–M–C* both extremes possess the same definiteness of economic form. Both are *commodities,* and of *equal value.* But at the same time they are qualitatively different use-values, and the process has social metabolism as its content. In *M–C–M* the operation, at first glance, seems tautological, purposeless. To exchange £100 for £100, and in a roundabout way to boot, seems absurd. One sum of money is distinguishable from another only by its *size; M–C–M* acquires its meaning, therefore, only through the *quantitative difference* in the extremes. More money is withdrawn from circulation than has been thrown into it. The cotton bought for £100 is sold, say, for £100+£10; the process thus follows the formula *M–C–M',* where $M'=M+\triangle M$. This $\triangle M$, *this increment is surplus-value.* The value originally advanced not only *remains intact* in circulation, but adds to itself a surplus-value, *expands itself*—and *this movement converts money into capital.*

In *C–M–C* there m a y also be a difference in the value of the extremes, but it is purely accidental in this form of circulation, and *C–M–C* does not become absurd when the extremes are equivalent—on the contrary, this is rather the necessary condition for the normal process.

The repetition of *C–M–C* is regulated by an ultimate object outside itself: consumption, the satisfaction of definite needs. In *M–C–M*, on the other hand, the beginning and the end are the same, money, and that already makes the movement endless. Granted, $M+\triangle M$ differs quantitatively from *M*, but it too is merely a *limited* sum of money; if it were spent, it would no longer be capital; if it were withdrawn from circulation, it would remain stationary as a hoard. Once the need for expansion of value is given, it exists for *M'* as well as for *M*, and the movement of capital is boundless, because its goal is as much unattained at the end of the process as at the beginning. (Pp. 111, 112 [149-51].) As the representative of this process, the owner of money becomes a *capitalist.*

If in commodity circulation the exchange-value attains at most a form independent of the use-value of commodities, *it*

*suddenly manifests itself here as a substance in process,
endowed with motion of its own, for which commodity and
money are mere forms. More than that, as original value it
is differentiated from itself as surplus-value.* It becomes
money in process, and as such, capital. (P. 116 [154].)

$M-C-M'$ appears indeed to be a form peculiar to merchant s capital alone. But industrial capital, too, is money
which is converted into commodities, and by the latter's sale
reconverted into more money. Acts that take place *between
purchase and sale, outside the sphere of circulation,* effect no
change in this. Lastly, in interest-bearing capital, the process
appears as $M-M'$ without any intermediary, value that is,
as it were, greater than itself. (P. 117 [155].)

2. CONTRADICTIONS
IN THE GENERAL FORMULA

The form of circulation by which money becomes capital
contradicts all previous laws bearing on the nature of commodities, of value, of money and of circulation itself. Can the
purely formal difference of inverted order of succession
cause this?

What is more, this inversion exists only for one of the
three transacting persons. As a capitalist I buy commodities
from A and sell them to B. A and B appear merely as simple
buyer and seller of commodities. In both cases I confront
them merely as a simple owner of money or owner of commodities, confronting one as buyer or money, the other as
seller or commodity, but neither of them as a capitalist or a
representative of something that is more than money or commodity. For A the transaction began with a *sale;* for B it
ended with a *purchase,* hence, just as in commodity circulation. Moreover, if I base the right to surplus-value upon the
simple sequence, A could sell to B directly and the chance
of surplus-value would be eliminated.

Assume that A and B buy commodities from each other
directly. As far as *use-value* is concerned, *both* may profit;
A may even produce more of his commodity than B could
produce in the same time, and *vice versa,* whereby both
would profit again. But otherwise with *exchange-value.* Here
equal values are exchanged for each other, even if money,
as the medium of circulation, intervenes. (P. 119 [156-58].)

Abstractly considered, only a *change in form* of the commodity takes place in simple commodity circulation, if we except the substitution of one use-value for another. So far as it involves only a change in form of its exchange-value, it involves the *exchange of equivalents*, if the phenomenon proceeds in a *pure* form. Commodities can, indeed, be sold at prices differing from their values, but this would mean a violation of the law of commodity exchange. In its pure form it is an exchange of equivalents, hence no medium for enriching oneself. (P. 120 [158-59].)

Hence the error of all endeavours to derive surplus-value from commodity circulation. Condillac (p. 121 [159]), Newman (p. 122 [160].)

But let us assume that the exchange does not take place in a pure form, that *non-equivalents are exchanged*. Let us assume that each seller sells his commodity at 10 per cent above its value. Everything remains the same; what each one gains as a seller, he loses in turn as a buyer. Just as if the value of money had changed by 10 per cent. Likewise if the *buyers* bought everything at 10 per cent *below* value. (P. 123 [160-61], Torrens.)

The assumption that surplus-value arises from a rise in prices presupposes that a class exists which *buys and does not sell, i.e., c o n s u m e s a n d d o e s n o t p r o d u c e,* which constantly receives money *gratis*. To sell commodities above their value to this class means merely to get back, by cheating, part of the money given away gratis. (Asia Minor and Rome). Yet the seller always remains the cheated one and cannot grow richer, cannot form surplus-value thereby.

Let us take the case of *c h e a t i n g. A* sells to *B* wine worth £40 in exchange for grain worth £50. *A* has gained £10. But *A* and *B* together have only 90. *A* has 50 and *B* only 40; value has been transferred but not *created*. The capitalist class, as a whole, in any country cannot cheat itself. (P. 126 [162-63].)

Hence: if equivalents are exchanged, no surplus-value results; and if non-equivalents are exchanged, still no surplus-value results. Commodity circulation creates no new value.

That is why the oldest and most popular forms of capital, merchant capital and usurers' capital, are not considered here. If the expansion of merchant capital is not to be explained by mere *cheating*, many intermediate factors, lacking here as yet, are required. Even more so for usurers' and interest-bearing capital. It will later be seen that both are derived forms, and why they occur historically *before* modern capital.

Hence surplus-value cannot originate in circulation. But outside it? Outside it the commodity owner is the simple producer of his commodity, the value of which depends upon the quantity of his own labour contained in it, measured according to a definite social law; this value is expressed in money of account, *e.g.*, in a price of £10. But this value is not at the same time a value of £11; his labour creates values, but not self-expanding values. It can add more value to existing value, but this occurs only through the addition of *more labour.* Thus the commodity producer *cannot produce surplus-value outside the sphere of circulation,* without coming in contact with other commodity owners.

Hence capital must originate *i n* commodity circulation and yet *n o t i n* it. (P. 128 [165-66].)

Thus: the transformation of money into capital has to be explained on the basis of the laws inherent to the exchange of commodities, the exchange of equivalents forming the starting point. Our owner of money, as yet the mere chrysalis of a capitalist, has to buy his commodities at their value, to sell them at their value, and yet at the end of this process to extract more value than he put into it. His development into a butterfly must take place in the sphere of circulation and yet not in it. These are the conditions of the problem. *Hic Rhodus, hic salta!* (P. 129[166].)

3. THE BUYING AND SELLING
OF LABOUR-POWER

The change in value of money that is to be converted into capital cannot take place in that money itself, for in buying, it merely realises the price of the commodity; and on the other hand, as long as it *remains money,* it does not change the magnitude of its value; and in selling, too, it merely converts the commodity from its bodily form into its money-form. The change must, therefore, take place in the *commodity* of M–C–M; but not in its *exchange-value,* since equivalents are exchanged; it can only arise from its *use-value as such,* that is, from its *consumption.* For that purpose a commodity is required *whose use-value possesses the property of being the source of exchange-value*—and this does exist—*l a b o u r -p o w e r.* (P. 130 [167].)

But for the owner of money to find labour-power in the market as a commodity, it must be sold by its own possessor, that is, it must be *f r e e* labour-power. Since buyer and seller as contracting parties are both *juridically equal* persons, labour-power must be sold only *temporarily*, since in a sale *en bloc* the seller no longer remains the seller, but becomes a commodity himself. But then the owner, instead of being able to sell *commodities* in which his labour is embodied, must rather be in a position where he has to sell *h i s l a b o u r-p o w e r   i t s e l f   a s   a   c o m m o d i t y.* (P. 131 [168-69].)

For the conversion of his money into capital, therefore, the owner of money must find in the commodity market the *free* labourer, free in the double sense that as a free man he can dispose of his labour-power as *his* commodity and that, on the other hand, he has no *other* commodities to sell, has no ties, is free of all *things* necessary for the realisation of his labour-power. (P. 132 [168-69].)

Parenthetically, the relation between money owner and labour-power owner is not a natural one, or a social one common to all ages, but a *historical* one, the product of many economic revolutions. So, too, do the economic categories considered up to now bear their historical stamp. To become a commodity, a product must no longer be produced as the immediate means of subsistence. The mass of products can assume commodity-form only *within a specific mode of production*, the *capitalist mode*, although commodity production and circulation can take place even where the mass of products never become commodities. Likewise, money can exist in all periods that have attained a certain level of commodity circulation; the specific money-forms, from mere equivalent to world money, presuppose various stages of development; nevertheless, a very slightly developed circulation of commodities can give rise to all of them. *Capital*, on the other hand, arises only under the above condition, and this one condition comprises a world's history. (P. 133 [169-70].)

Labour-power has an exchange-value which is determined, like that of all other commodities, by the labour-time required for its production, and hence for its reproduction as well. The value of labour-power is the value of the means of subsistence necessary for the maintenance of its owner, that is, his maintenance in a state of normal capacity for work. This depends upon *climate, natural conditions*, etc., and also on the given *historical* standard of life in each country. These vary, but they are *given* for each particular country and for each particular epoch. Moreover, his maintenance includes the means of subsistence for his *substitutes, i.e.*, his *children*, in order that the race of these peculiar commodity owners may perpetuate itself. Furthermore, for skilled labour, the cost of *education*. (P. 135 [170-72].)

The minimum limit of the value of labour-power is the value of *the physically indispensable means of subsistence*. If the price of labour-power falls to this minimum, it falls below its *value*, since the latter presupposes *normal*, not stunted, quality of labour-power. (P. 136 [173].)

The nature of labour implies that labour-power is consumed only *after* conclusion of the contract, and, as money is usually the *means of payment* for such commodities in all countries with the capitalist mode of production, the labour-power is paid for only after it is *consumed*. Everywhere, therefore, *the labourer gives credit to the capitalist*. (Pp. 137, 138 [174].)

The process of consuming labour-power is at the same time *the process of producing commodities and surplus-value* and this consumption takes place outside *the sphere of circulation*. (P. 140 [175-76].)

CHAPTER III

THE PRODUCTION
OF ABSOLUTE SURPLUS-VALUE

1. THE LABOUR PROCESS AND THE PROCESS
OF PRODUCING SURPLUS-VALUE

The purchaser of labour-power consumes it by setting its seller to work. This labour to produce commodities at first turns out use-values, and in this property it is independent of the specific relation between capitalist and labourer.... Description of the labour process as such. (Pp. 141-49 [177-85].)

The labour process, on a capitalist basis, has two peculiarities. 1. The labourer works under the capitalist's control. 2. The product is the capitalist's property, since the labour process is now only a process between two *things* purchased by the capitalist: labour-power and means of production. (P. 150 [184-85].)

But the capitalist does not want the use-value produced *for its own sake*, but only as the depository of *exchange-value* and especially of *surplus-value*. Labour under this condition—where the commodity was a unity of use-value and exchange-value—becomes the *unity of the production process and of the process of creating value*. (P. 151 [186].)

Thus the quantity of labour embodied in the product is to be investigated.

Yarn, for example. Let 10 lbs. of cotton be necessary for making it, say 10 shillings, and instruments of labour, whose wear and tear are inevitable in the spinning—here denoted in brief as spindle share—say 2 shillings. Thus, there are 12 shillings' worth of means of production in the product, *i.e.*, inasmuch as 1) the product has become *an actual use-value*, in this case yarn; and 2) *only* the socially necessary labour-time was represented in these instruments of labour. How much is added to it by the labour of spinning?

The labour process is here viewed from an altogether different angle. In the value of the product the labours of the cotton-planter, of the spindle-maker, etc., and of the spinner, are commensurable, qualitatively equal parts of general, human, necessary *value-creating* labour, and therefore distinguishable only quantitatively, and for that very reason *quantitatively comparable* by the length of time, presupposing that it is *socially necessary* labour-time, for only the latter is value-creating.

Assumed the value of a day's labour-power is 3 shillings, and that it represents 6 hours of labour, that $1\frac{2}{3}$ lbs. of yarn are made per hour, hence in 6 hours: 10 lbs. of yarn from 10 lbs. of cotton (as above); then 3 shillings of value have been added in 6 hours, and the value of the product is 15 shillings (10+2+3 shillings) or a shilling and a half per pound of yarn.

But in this case there is no surplus-value. This is of no use to the capitalist. (Vulgar-economic humbug, p. 157 [190].)

We assumed that the value of a day's labour-power was 3 shillings, because $\frac{1}{2}$ working-day, or 6 hours, is incorporated in it. *But the fact that only $\frac{1}{2}$ working-day is required to maintain the worker for 24 hours does not in any way prevent him from working a whole day.* The *value* of labour-power and *the value it creates* are two different quantities. Its *useful* property was only a *conditio sine qua non*; but what was decisive was the *specific* use-value of labour-power *in being the source of more exchange-value than it has itself.* (P. 159 [193].)

Hence, the labourer works 12 hours, spins 20 lbs. of cotton worth 20 shillings and 4 shillings' worth of spindles, and his labour costs 3 shillings: total–27 shillings. But in the product there are embodied: four days' labour in the shape of spindles and cotton, and one day's labour of the spinner, in all five days at 6 shillings totalling *30 shillings' value of product. We have a surplus-value of 3 shillings: money has been converted into capital.* (P. 160 [194].) All the conditions of the problem are fulfilled. (Details p. 160 [194].)

As a value-creating process, the labour process becomes a *process of producing surplus-value* the moment it is *prolonged beyond* the point where it delivers a simple *equivalent* for the paid-for value of labour-power.

The value-creating process differs from the simple labour process in that the latter is considered *qualitatively*, the former *quantitatively*, and only to the extent that it comprises socially necessary labour-time. (P. 161 [195], details p. 162 [196].)

As the unity of labour process and *value-creating process*, the production process is the *production of commodities*; as the unity of labour process and the *process of producing surplus-value* it is the *process of capitalist production of commodities.* (P. 163 [197].)

Reduction of compound labour to simple labour. (Pp. 163-65 [197-98].)

2. CONSTANT AND VARIABLE CAPITAL

The labour process adds *new* value to the object of labour, but at the same time it *transfers* the value of the object of labour to the product, thus *preserving* it by merely adding

70

new value. This double result is attained in this manner: the *specifically useful qualitative character* of labour converts one use-value into another use-value and *thus preserves value;* the *value-creating, abstractly general, quantitative character* of labour, however, *adds value.* (P. 166 [199].)

E.g., let the productivity of spinning labour multiply sixfold. As *useful* (qualitative) labour it *preserves* in the same time six times as many instruments of labour. But it adds only the same *new* value as before, i.e., in each pound of yarn there is only $\frac{1}{6}$ of the new value previously added. As *value-creating* labour it accomplishes no more than before. (P. 167 [201].) The contrary is true, if the productivity of spinning labour remains the same, but the value of the instruments of labour rises. (P. 168 [201].)

The instruments of labour transfer to the product only *that* value which they *lose themselves.* (P. 169 [203].) This is the case in differing degree. Coal, lubricants, etc., are consumed completely, raw materials take on a new form. Instruments, machinery, etc., transmit value only slowly and by parts, and the wear and tear are calculated by experience. (Pp. 169-70 [203].) But the instrument remains continually *as a whole* in the labour process. Therefore, the same instrument counts *as a whole in the labour process* but only partly in the *process of producing surplus-value,* so that the difference between the two processes is reflected here in material factors. (P. 171 [204].) Conversely, the raw material, which forms waste, enters wholly into the process of producing surplus-value, and only partly into the labour process, since it appears in the product minus the waste. (P. 171 [205].)

But in no case can an instrument of labour transfer *more* exchange-value than it possessed itself—in the labour process it acts only as a use-value and hence can give only the exchange-value that it possessed previously. (P. 172 [205-06].)

This preserving of value is very advantageous to the capitalist but costs him nothing. (Pp. 173, 174 [205, 207].)

Yet the preserved *value only re-appears,* it was already present, and only the labour process *adds new value.* That is, in capitalist production, *surplus-value, the excess of the product's value over the value of the consumed elements of the product* (means of production and labour-power). (Pp. 175, 176 [208].)

Herewith have been described the forms of existence which the original capital value takes on in dropping its money-form, in being converted into factors of the labour process: (1) in the purchase of *instruments of labour*; (2) in the purchase of *labour-power*.

The capital invested in *instruments* of labour does *not* therefore alter the magnitude of its value in the production process. We call it *constant capital*.

The portion invested in labour-*power does change* its value; it produces: 1) its *own* value, and 2) *surplus*-value—it is *variable capital*. (P. 176 [209].)

Capital is *constant* only in relation to the production process specifically given, in which it does not change; it can consist sometimes of more, sometimes of fewer instruments of labour, and the purchased instruments of labour may rise or fall in value, but that does not affect their relationship to the production process. (P. 177 [210-11].) Likewise, the percentage in which a given capital is subdivided into constant and variable capital may change, but in any given case the *c* remains constant and the *v* variable. (P. 178 [211].)

3. THE RATE OF SURPLUS-VALUE

$$\overset{c}{C}=£500=\overset{c}{410}+\overset{v}{90}.$$ At the end of the labour process in which *v* is turned into labour-power we get $\overset{c}{410}+\overset{v}{90}+\overset{s}{90}=590$. Let us assume *c* consists of 312 raw material, 44 auxiliary material, and 54 wear and tear of machinery, in all 410. Let the value of *all* the machinery be 1,054. If this were entered as a *whole*, we would get 1,410 for *c* on both sides of our calculation; the surplus-value would remain 90 as before. (P. 179 [212].)

Since the value of *c* merely *re-appears* in the product, the *value of the product* we get differs from the *value* created in the process; the latter, therefore, equals not $c+v+s$, but $v+s$. Hence the magnitude of *c* is immaterial to the process of creating surplus-value, *i.e.*, $c=0$. (P. 180 [213].) This also takes place in practice in commercial accounting, *e.g.*, in calculating a country's profit from its industry, imported raw material is deducted. (P. 181 [215].) *Cf.* Vol. III for the ratio of surplus-value to total capital.

Hence: the rate of surplus-value is $s : v$, in the above case 90 : 90=100%.

The labour-time during which the labourer reproduces the value of his labour-power—in capitalist or other circumstances —is the *necessary* labour; what goes beyond that, producing surplus-value for the capitalist, *surplus-labour.* (Pp. 183, 184 [215, 217].) Surplus-value is congealed surplus-labour, and only the *form of extorting* the same differentiates the various social formations.

Example of the incorrectness of including *c*, pp. 185-96 [217-29] (*Senior.*)

The sum of the necessary labour and the surplus-labour equals the *working-day.*

4. THE WORKING-DAY

The *necessary* labour-time is *given.* The *surplus*-labour is *variable,* but within certain limits. It can never be reduced to nil, since then capitalist production ceases. It can never go as high as 24 hours for physical reasons, and, moreover, the maximum limit is always affected by moral grounds as well. But these limits are very elastic. The economic demand is that the working-day should be no longer than for normal wear and tear of the worker. But what is *normal?* An antinomy results and only force can decide. Hence the struggle between the working class and the capitalist class for the *normal working-day.* (Pp. 198-202 [231-35].)

Surplus-labour in previous social epochs. As long as the exchange-value is not more important than the use-value, surplus-labour is milder, *e.g.,* among the ancients; only where direct exchange-value—gold and silver—was produced, surplus-labour was terrible. (P. 203 [235].) Likewise in the slave states of America until the mass production of cotton for export. Likewise *corvée* labour, *e.g.,* in Rumania.

Corvée labour is the best means of comparison with capitalist exploitation, because the former fixes and shows the surplus-labour as a specific labour-time to be performed —*Reglement organique* of Wallachia. (Pp. 204-06 [235-36].)

The English *Factory Acts* are negative expression of the greed for surplus-labour, just as the foregoing was its positive expression.

The Factory Acts. That of 1850—(p. 207 [239]). 10$\frac{1}{2}$ hours and $7^1/_2$ on Saturdays=60 hours per week. Mill-owners' profit through evasion. (Pp. 208-11 [240-43].)

Exploitation in *unrestricted* or only later restricted branches: *lace industry* (p. 212 [243]), *potteries* (p. 213 [244]), *lucifer matches* (p. 214 [246]), *wall-paper* (pp. 214-17 [246-48]), *baking* (pp. 217-22 [248-51]), *railway employees* (p. 223 [253]), *seamstresses* (pp. 223-25 [254-56]), *blacksmiths* (p. 226 [256]), *day and night workers in shifts*: (a) *metallurgy and the metal industry* (pp. 227-35 [256-63]).

These facts prove that capital regards the labourer as nothing else than *labour-power*, all of whose time is labour-time as far as this is at all possible at a given moment, and that the length of life of labour-power is immaterial to the capitalists. (Pp. 236-38 [264-65].) But is this not against the interests of the capitalist? What about the replacement of what is rapidly worn out? The organised slave trade in the interior of the United States has raised the rapid wearing out of slaves to an economic principle, exactly like the supply of labourers from the rural districts in Europe, etc. (P. 239 [267].) Poorhouse supply (labour-power provided by poorhouses). (P. 240 [267].) The capitalist sees only the continuously available surplus-population and wears it out. Whether the race perishes—*après moi le déluge. Capital is reckless of the health or length of life of the labourer, unless under compulsion from society ... and free competition brings out the inherent laws of capitalist production in the shape of external coercive laws having power over every individual capitalist.* (P. 243 [270].)

Establishment of a normal working-day—the result of centuries of struggle between capitalist and labourer.

At the beginning laws were made to *raise* working-time; now to lower it. (P. 244 [271].) The first Statute of Labourers, 23rd Edward III, 1349, was passed under the pretext that the plague had so decimated the population that everyone had to do more work. Hence maximum wages and limit of the working-day were fixed by law. In 1496, under Henry VII, the working day of field labourers and all artificers continued from 5 a.m. to between 7 and 8 p.m. in summer—March to September, with 1 hour, $1^1/_2$ hours and $^1/_2$ hour, in all 3 hours' break. In winter it was from 5 a.m. to dark. This statute was never strictly enforced. In the 18th century the *whole* week's labour was not yet available to capital (with the exception of agricultural labour). *Cf.* controversies of that time. (Pp. 248-51 [274-77].) Only with modern large-scale industry was this, and more, achieved; it broke down *all* bounds and exploited the workers most shamelessly. The proletariat resisted as soon as it recollected itself. The five acts of 1802-33 were only nominal, since there were no inspectors. Only the Act of 1833 created a normal working-day in the four textile industries: from 5.30 a.m. to 8.30 p.m., during which time young persons from 13 to 18 years of age could be employed only 12 hours with $1\frac{1}{2}$ hours' pause, children from 9 to 13 years of age only 8 hours, while night work of children and juveniles was prohibited. (Pp. 253-55 [278-80].)

The *relay system* and its abuse for purposes of evasion. (P. 256 [281].) Finally, the Act of 1844 which put *women of all ages* on the same basis as juveniles. Children limited to $6\frac{1}{2}$ hours; the relay system curbed. On the other hand, children permitted from *8 years* on. At last in 1847 the *ten-hour bill* forced through for women and juveniles. (P. 259 [283].) The capitalists' efforts against it. (Pp. 260-68 [283-92].) A flaw in the Act of 1847 led to the compromise Act of 1850 (p. 269 [292]), which fixed the working-day for juveniles and women—5 days of $10\frac{1}{2}$, 1 day of $7\frac{1}{2}=60$ hours per week, and that *between 6 a.m. and 6 p.m.* Otherwise the Act of 1847 in force for children. The exception for the silk industry. (*Cf.* p. 270 [293].) In 1853 the working-time *for children* also limited to between 6 a.m. and 6 p.m. (P. 272 [294].)

Printworks Act in 1845 limits almost nothing—children and women can work 16 hours!

Bleaching and dyeing works 1860. Lace factories 1861; potteries and many other branches 1863 (under the Factory Act, special acts passed the same year for bleaching in the open air and baking). (P. 274 [296-97].)

Large-scale industry thus at first creates the need for limiting working-time, but it is later found that the same overwork has gradually taken possession of all other branches as well. (P. 277 [298].)

History further shows that the *isolated* "free" labourer is defenceless against the capitalist and succumbs, especially with the introduction of women's and children's labour, so that it is here that the class struggle develops between the workers and the capitalists. (P. 278 [299].)

In France, the twelve-hour day law for all ages and

branches of work was passed only in 1848. (*Cf.*, however, p. 253 [278], footnote on the French child labour law of 1841, which was really enforced only in 1853, and only in the *Département du Nord*.) Complete "freedom of labour" in Belgium. The eight-hour movement in America. (P. 279 [301].)

Thus, the labourer comes out of the production process quite different than he entered. The labour contract was not the act of a *free agent*; the time for which he *is free* to sell his labour-power is the time for which he *is forced* to sell it, and only the *mass* opposition of the workers wins for them *the passing of a law* that shall prevent the workers from selling, by voluntary contract with capital, themselves and their generation into slavery and death. In place of the pompous catalogue of the inalienable rights of man comes the modest *Magna Charta* of the Factory Act. (Pp. 280, 281 [302].)

5. RATE AND MASS OF SURPLUS-VALUE

With the *rate*, the *mass* is also given. If the daily value of one labour-power is 3 shillings, and the rate of surplus-value is 100 per cent, its daily mass=3 shillings for one labourer.

I. Since the *variable capital* is the money expression of the value of *all* the labour-powers simultaneously employed by one capitalist, the mass of the surplus-value produced by them is equal to the variable capital multiplied by the rate of surplus-value. Both factors can vary, different combinations thus arising. The *mass* of surplus-value can grow, even with decreasing variable capital, if the rate rises, that is, if the working-day is *lengthened*. (P. 282 [303-05].)

II. This increase in the rate of surplus-value has its *absolute limit* in that the working-day can never be prolonged to the full 24 hours; hence the total value of *one* worker's daily production can *never* equal the value of 24 working-hours. Thus, in order to obtain the *same* mass of surplus-value, variable capital can be replaced by increased exploitation of labour only *within these limits*. This is important for the explanation of various phenomena arising from the contradictory tendency of capital: (1) to *reduce* the variable capital and the number of workers employed; and (2) to produce the greatest possible mass of surplus-value nonetheless. (Pp. 283, 284 [305-06].)

III. The masses of value and surplus-value produced by different capitals, for given value and equally high degree of exploitation of labour-power, *are related directly as the magnitudes of the variable components of these capitals.* (P. 285 [306-07].) This seems to contradict all facts.

For a given society and a given working-day, surplus-value can be increased only by increasing the number of workers, *i.e.*, the population; with a given number of workers, only by lengthening the working-day. This is important, however, only for *absolute* surplus-value.

It now turns out that not *every* sum of money can be transformed into capital—that a minimum exists: the cost price of *a single* labour-power and of the necessary instruments of labour. In order to be able to live like a worker, the capitalist would have to have two workers, with a rate of surplus-value of 50 per cent, and yet save nothing. Even with eight he is still a small master. Hence, in the Middle Ages people were forcibly hampered in transformation from craftsmen into capitalists by limitation of the number of journeymen to be employed by one master. The minimum of wealth required to form a real capitalist varies in different periods and branches of business. (P. 288 [309].)

Capital has evolved into *command over labour,* and sees to it that work is done regularly and intensively. Moreover, it *compels* the workers to do more work than is necessary for their sustenance; and in pumping out surplus-labour it surpasses all earlier production systems based upon *direct* compulsory labour.

Capital takes over labour with the given technical conditions, and at first does not change them. Hence, with the production process considered as a *labour process,* the worker stands in relation to the means of production not as to capital, but as to the means of his own intelligent activity. But, considered as a process of *creating surplus-value,* otherwise. The means of production become means of *absorbing the labour of others.* It is *no longer the labourer who employs the means of production, but the means of production that employ the labourer.* (P. 289 [310].) Instead of being consumed *by him . . . they consume him* as the ferment necessary to their own life-process, and the life-process of capital consists only in its movement *as value constantly multiplying itself. . . .* The simple transformation of money into means of production transforms the latter into *a title* and a right *to the labour and surplus-labour of others.*

CHAPTER IV

THE PRODUCTION
OF RELATIVE SURPLUS-VALUE

1. THE CONCEPT OF RELATIVE SURPLUS VALUE

For a given working-day, surplus-labour can be increased only by reducing the *necessary* labour; this can in turn be obtained—apart from lowering wages below value—only by reducing the value of labour, that is, by reducing the price of the necessary means of subsistence. (Pp. 291-93 [312-15].) This, in turn, is to be attained only by *increasing the productive power of labour, by revolutionising the mode of production itself.*

The surplus-value produced by lengthening the working-day is *absolute*, that produced by shortening the necessary labour-time is *relative* surplus-value. (P. 295 [315].)

In order to lower the value of labour, the increase in productive power must seize upon those branches of industry whose products determine the value of labour-power—ordinary means of subsistence, substitutes for the same, and their raw materials, etc. Proof of how competition makes the increased productive power manifest in a lower commodity price. (Pp. 296-99 [316-19].)

The *value* of commodities is in *inverse ratio* to the productivity of labour, as is also *the value of labour-power*, because it depends on the price of commodities. *Relative surplus-value*, on the contrary, is *directly proportional* to the productivity of labour. (P. 299 [319].)

The capitalist is not interested in the *absolute* value of commodities, but only in the *surplus-value* incorporated in them. Realisation of surplus-value implies refunding of the value advanced. Since, according to p. 299 [320], the same process of increasing productive power lowers the value of commodities and increases the surplus-value contained in them, it is clear why the capitalist, whose sole concern is the production of exchange-value, continually strives to depress the exchange-value of commodities. (*Cf.* Quesnay, p. 300 [320].)

Hence in capitalist production, economising labour through developing productive power by no means aims at shortening the working-day—the latter may even be *lengthened*. We may read, therefore, in economists of the stamp of McCulloch, Ure, Senior and *tutti quanti*, on one page *that the labourer owes a debt of gratitude to capital for developing the productive forces*, and on the next page *that he must prove his gratitude by working in future for 15 hours instead of 10.* The object of this development of productive forces is only to shorten the *necessary labour* and to lengthen the labour for the capitalist. (P. 301 [321].)

2. CO-OPERATION

According to p. 288 [309], capitalist production requires an individual capital big enough to employ a fairly large number of workers at a time; only when he himself is wholly released from labour does the employer of labour become a full-grown capitalist. The activity of a large number of workers, at the same time, in the same field of work, for the production of the same kind of commodity, under the command of the same capitalist, constitutes, *historically and logically, the starting point of capitalist production.* (P. 302 [322].)

At first, therefore, there is only a *quantitative* difference compared to the past, when *fewer* labourers were employed by one employer. But a modification takes place at once. The large number of labourers already guarantees that the employer gets *real average labour*, which is not the case with the small master, who must pay the average value of labour none the less; in the case of small production, the inequalities are compensated for society at large, but not for the individual master. Thus the *law of the production of surplus-value* is fully realised for the individual producer only when he produces *as a capitalist*, and sets many labourers to work at the same time—hence *from the outset average social labour.* (Pp. 303-04 [322-24].)

Moreover: economy in means of production is achieved through large-scale operation alone; less transfer of value to the product by constant capital components, arises solely from their joint consumption in the labour process of many workmen. That is how the *instruments* of labour acquire a social character before the labour *process* itself does so (up to this time merely similar processes side by side). (P. 305 [325].)

The economy in the means of production is to be considered here only in so far as it cheapens commodities and thus lowers *the value of labour*. The extent to which it alters the ratio of surplus-value to the *total capital* advanced ($c+v$) will not be considered until Book III. This splitting up is quite in keeping with the spirit of capitalist production; since it makes the working conditions confront the worker independently, economy in the means of production appears to be a distinct operation, which does not concern him and has therefore no connection with the methods by which the productivity of the labour-power consumed by the capitalist is increased.

The form of labour of many persons, methodically working together and alongside one another in the same production process or in related production processes, is called co-operation. (P. 306 [325].) (*Concours des forces.* Destutt de Tracy.)

The sum-total of the mechanical forces of individual workers differs substantially from the *potential* mechanical *force* developed when many hands *act together* at one time in the same undivided operation (lifting of weight, etc.). Co-operation, from the very start, creates a productive power that is, in itself, a *mass power*.

Furthermore, in most productive work, *mere social contact* creates a *spirit of emulation* which raises the individual efficiency of each, so that 12 workers turn out more work in a joint working-day of 144 hours than 12 workers in 12 distinct working-days, or one worker in 12 successive days. (P. 307 [326].)

Although many may be doing the same or similar things, the individual labour of each may still represent a different phase of the labour process (chain of persons passing something along), whereby co-operation again saves labour. Likewise, when a building is started from several sides at once. The combined worker, or collective worker, has hands and eyes before and behind and is, to a certain degree, omnipresent. (P. 308 [327].)

In complicated labour processes co-operation permits the

special processes to be distributed and to be done simultaneously, thus shortening the labour-time for manufacturing the whole product. (P. 308 [327].)

In many spheres of production there are *critical periods* when many workers are needed (harvesting, herring catches, etc.). Here only co-operation can be of aid. (P. 309 [328].)

On the one hand, co-operation extends the field of production and thus becomes a necessity for work requiring great spatial continuity of the working arena (drainage, road-building, dam construction, etc.); on the other hand, it *contracts* the arena by concentrating the workers in one work-place, thus cutting down costs. (P. 310 [328-29].)

In all these forms, co-operation is the specific productive power of the combined working-day, social productive power of labour. The latter arises from co-operation itself. In systematic joint work with others, the worker sheds his individual limitations and develops the capabilities of his species.

Now, wage-labourers cannot co-operate unless *the same capitalist* employs them simultaneously, pays them and provides them with instruments of labour. Hence the scale of co-operation depends upon *how much capital a capitalist has.* The requirement that a certain amount of capital be present to make its owner a capitalist now becomes the *material* condition for the conversion of the numerous dispersed and independent labour processes into one combined social labour process.

In a like manner, capital's *command* over labour was up to now only the formal result of the relation between capitalist and labourer; now it is the *necessary prerequisite* for the labour process itself; the capitalist represents combination in the labour process. In co-operation, *control* of the labour process becomes the *function of capital,* and as such it acquires specific characteristics. (P. 312 [330].)

In accordance with the aim of capitalist production (the greatest possible self-expansion of capital), this control is at the same time the function of the greatest possible exploitation of a social labour process, and hence involves the inevitable antagonism between exploiter and exploited. Moreover, control of proper utilisation of the instruments of labour. Finally, the connection between the various workers' functions lies *outside them,* in capital, so that their own unity confronts them as *the capitalist's authority*, as an outside will. Capitalist control is thus *twofold* (1. a social labour process for producing a product; 2. a process of self-expansion of capital), and in its form *despotic*. This despotism now evolves its own peculiar forms: the capitalist, just relieved from actual labour himself, now hands over immediate supervision to an organised band of officers and noncoms, who themselves are wage-labourers of capital. In *slavery*, the economists count these supervision expenses as *faux frais*, but in capitalist production they bluntly identify control, so far as it is conditioned by exploitation, with the same function, so far as it arises from the nature of the social labour process. (Pp. 313, 314 [331, 332].)

The leadership of industry becomes the attribute of capital, just as in feudal times the functions of general and judge were attributes of landed property. (P. 314 [332].)

The capitalist buys 100 individual labour-powers, and gets in return a combined labour-power of 100. He does *not* pay for the combined labour-power of the 100, When the labourers enter the combined labour process, they already cease to belong to themselves; they are incorporated in capital. Thus the *social productive power of labour* appears as the *productive power immanent in capital*. (P. 315 [333].)

Examples of co-operation among the ancient Egyptians. (P. 316 [333-34].)

Primitive co-operation at the beginnings of civilisation, among hunting peoples, nomads, or in Indian communities, is based: (1) on common ownership of the means of production; (2) on the natural attachment of the individual to the tribe and the primeval community. The sporadic co-operation in antiquity, the Middle Ages, and in modern colonies is based upon direct rule and violence, mostly slavery. Capitalist co-operation, on the contrary, presupposes the free wage-labourer. Historically, it appears in direct opposition to peasant economy and the independent handicrafts (whether in guilds or not), and in this connection, as a historical form peculiar to, and distinguishing, the capitalist production process. It is the first change experienced by the labour process when subjected to capital. Thus, here at once: (1) the capitalist mode of production presents itself as a historical condition for the transformation of the labour process into a social process; (2) this social form of the labour process presents itself as a method of capital to exploit labour more profitably by increasing its productivity. (P. 317 [335].)

Co-operation, as considered so far, in its *elementary* form, coincides with production on a larger scale, but it does not constitute a fixed form characteristic of a particular epoch, of capitalist production, and it still exists today, when capital operates on a large scale without division of labour or machinery playing an important part. Thus, although co-operation is the basic form of the whole capitalist production, its *elementary* form appears as a particular form alongside its more developed forms. (P. 318 [335].)

3. DIVISION OF LABOUR AND MANUFACTURE

Manufacture, the classic form of co-operation based upon division of labour, prevails from about 1550 to 1770. It arises:

(1) Either through the assemblage of different crafts, each of which performs a detail operation (*e.g.*, vehicle building), whereby the individual craftsman very soon loses his ability to pursue his *whole* handicraft, on the other hand doing his detail work so much better; and thus the process is converted into a division of the whole operation into its component parts. (Pp. 318, 319 [336, 337].)

(2) Or many craftsmen doing the same or similar work are united in the same factory, and the individual processes, instead of being performed successively by one worker, are gradually separated and done simultaneously by several workers. (Needles, etc.) Instead of being the work of one artificer, the product is now the work of a union of artificers, each of whom performs only a detail operation. (Pp. 319, 320 [337, 338].)

In both cases their result is a *productive mechanism whose organs are human beings.* The work retains a *handicraft nature*; each detail process through which the product goes must be performable *by hand*; hence any *really scientific analysis of the production process is excluded.* Each individual worker is completely chained to a detail function *because* of its handicraft nature. (P. 321 [338-39].)

In this way labour is saved, as compared to the craftsman, and this is increased still more by transmission to succeeding generations. Thus the division of labour in manufacture corresponds to the tendency of former societies to make a trade hereditary. Castes, guilds. (P. 322 [339-40].)

Subdivision of tools through adaptation to the various partial operations—500 kinds of hammers in Birmingham. (Pp. 323-24 [341].)

Manufacture, considered from the standpoint of its *total* mechanism, has two aspects: either merely mechanical assembly of independent detail products (watch), or a series of related processes in *one* workshop (needle).

In manufacture, each group of workers supplies another with its raw material. Hence the basic condition is that each group *produces a given quantum in a given time;* thus a continuity, regularity, uniformity and intensity of labour of quite a different kind are created than in co-operation proper. *Thus here we have the t e c h n i c a l law of the p r o d u c t i o n p r o c e s s: that the labour be socially necessary labour.* (P. 329 [345].)

The inequality of the time required for the individual operations makes it necessary that the different groups of workers be of different *size* and number (in type founding: four founders and two breakers to one rubber). Thus manufacture sets up a mathematically fixed ratio for the quantitative extent of the several organs of the collective worker, and production can be expanded only by employing an additional *multiple* of the whole group. Moreover, only after a definite level of production has been reached does it pay to make certain functions independent: supervision, transporting the products from place to place, etc. (Pp. 329, 330 [346].)

Combination of various manufactures into a united manufacture also occurs, but as yet it always lacks real technical unity, which arises only with machinery. (P. 331 [347-48].)

Machines appeared in manufacture at an early date—sporadically—grain and stamping mills, etc., but only as something subordinate. The chief machinery of manufacture is the *combined collective worker,* who possesses a much higher degree of perfection than the old individual craft worker, and in whom all the imperfections, such as are often necessarily developed in the detail worker, appear as perfection. (P. 333 [348-49].) Manufacture evolves differences among these detail workers, skilled and unskilled, and even a complete hierarchy of workers. (P. 334 [349].)

Division of labour: 1) general (into agriculture, industry, shipping, etc.); 2) particular (into species and subspecies); 3) in detail (in the workshop). The social division of labour also develops from different starting points. 1) Within the family and the tribe the natural division of labour according to sex and age, plus slavery through violence against neighbours, which extends it. (P. 335 [351-52].) 2) Different communities according to location, climate, and level of culture, turn out different products which are *exchanged where these communities come in contact*. (P. 49 [87].) Exchange with foreign communities is then one of the chief means of breaking off the natural association of the community itself through further development of the natural division of labour. (P. 336 [352].)

Division of labour in manufacture thus presupposes a certain degree of development of the social division of labour; on the other hand, it develops the latter further—as in the territorial division of labour. (Pp. 337, 338 [352, 353].)

For all that, there is always this difference between social division of labour and division of labour in manufacture that the former necessarily produces *commodities*, whereas in the latter the detail worker does *not* produce commodities. Hence concentration and organisation in the latter, scattering and disorder of competition in the former. (Pp. 339, 341 [354, 356].)

Earlier organisation of the Indian communities. (Pp. 341, 342 [357].) The guild. (Pp. 343-44 [358-59].) Whereas in all these there exists division of labour in *society*, the division of labour in manufacture is a *specific creation of the capitalist mode of production*.

As in co-operation, the functioning working organism is a *form of existence of capital* in manufacture as well. Hence the productive power arising from the combination of labours appears to be the *productive power of capital*. But whereas co-operation leaves the individual's mode of working on the whole unchanged, manufacture revolutionises it, cripples the worker; unable to make a product independently, he is now a mere *appendage* of the capitalist's workshop. The intellectual faculties of labour disappear as far as the many are concerned, to expand in scope for the one. It is a result of the division of labour in manufacture that the labourers *are brought face to face* with the intellectual potencies of the labour process as *the property of another and as a ruling power*. This process of separation, which begins as early as co-operation and develops in manufacture, is completed in modern industry, which separates science as an independent productive force from labour and presses it into the service of capital. (P. 346 [361].)

Illustrative quotations. (P. 347 [362-63].)

Manufacture, in one aspect a definite organisation of social labour, is in another only a particular *method of begetting relative surplus-value*. (P. 350 [364].) Historical significance *ibidem*.

Obstacles to the development of manufacture even during its classical period are limitation of the number of unskilled workers owing to the predominance of the skilled; limitation of the work of women and children owing to the men's resistance; the insistence on the laws of apprenticeship up to recent times, even where superfluous; continual insubordination of the workers, since the collective worker as yet possesses no framework independent of the workers; emigration of the workers. (Pp. 353, 354 [367, 368].)

Besides, manufacture itself was unable to revolutionise the whole of social production or even merely to dominate it. Its narrow technical basis came into conflict with the production requirements that it had itself created. The machine became necessary, and manufacture had already learned how to make it. (P. 355 [368].)

4. MACHINERY AND MODERN INDUSTRY

a. Machinery as Such

The revolution in the mode of production, starting in manufacture with labour-*power*, here starts with the *instruments* of labour.

All fully-developed machinery consists of 1) the motor mechanism; 2) the transmitting mechanism; 3) the tool or working machine. (P. 357 [373].)

The industrial revolution of the eighteenth century started with the *working machine*. What characterises it is that the tool—in a more or less modified form—is transferred from man to the machine, and is worked by the machine under the operation of man. At the outset it is immaterial whether the motive *power* is human or a natural one. The specific difference is that man *uses* only his *own organs while the machine can, within certain limits, employ as many tools as demanded.* (Spinning-wheel, 1 spindle; jenny, 12 to 18 spindles.)

So far, in the spinning-wheel it is not the treadle, the power, but the spindle that is affected by the industrial revolution —at the beginning man is still motive power and tender at the same time everywhere. The revolution of the working machine, on the contrary, first made the perfecting of the steam-engine a necessity, and then also carried it out. (Pp. 359-60 [374-75]; also pp. 361-62 [376-77].)

Two kinds of machinery in modern industry: either (1) co-operation of similar machines (power-loom, envelope-machine, which combines the work of a number of detail workers through the combination of various tools), in this case technical oneness already, through the transmission and the motive power; or 2) machine system, combination of different detail machines (spinning-mill). The natural basis for this is the division of labour in manufacture. But at once an essential difference. In manufacture every detail process had to be adapted to the *labourer;* this is no longer necessary here —the labour process can be *objectively* dissected into its component parts, which are then left to science, or to experience based upon it, to be mastered by machines. Here the quantitative ratio of the several groups of workers is repeated as the ratio of the several groups of machines. (Pp. 363-66 [378-79].)

In both cases the factory constitutes a *big automaton* (moreover perfected to that stage only recently) and this is its adequate form. (P. 367 [379].) And its most perfect form is the *machine-building automaton,* which abolished the handicraft and manufacture foundation of large-scale industry, and thus first provided the consummate form of machinery. (Pp. 369-72 [384-86].)

Connection between the revolutionising of the various branches, up to the means of communication. (P. 371 [383].)

In manufacture the combination of workers is subjective. Here there is an objective *mechanical* production organism, which the worker finds ready at hand, and which can function only through collective labour; the co-operative character of the labour process is now a *technical necessity*. (P. 372 [386].)

The productive forces arising from co-operation and the division of labour cost capital nothing; the natural forces: steam, water, also cost nothing. Neither do the forces discovered by science. But the latter can be realised only with suitable apparatus, which can be constructed only at great expense; likewise the working machines cost much more than the old tools. But these machines have a much longer life and a much greater field of production than the tool; they therefore transfer a much smaller portion of value, comparatively, to the product than a tool, and hence the *gratuitous service* performed by the machine (which does *not* re-appear in the value of the product) is much greater than in the case of the tool. (Pp. 374, 375, 376 [387, 388, 390].)

Reduction in cost through concentration of production is much greater in modern industry than in manufacture. (P. 375 [388].)

The prices of finished goods prove how much the machine has cheapened production, and that the portion of value due to the instruments of labour grows relatively but declines absolutely. The productivity of the machine is measured by the extent to which it *replaces human labour-power*. Examples (pp. 377-79 [390-92].)

Assumed a steam plough takes the place of 150 workers getting an annual wage of £3,000, this annual wage does *not* represent *all the labour performed by them*, but only the *necessary* labour—however, they also perform *surplus-labour* in addition. If the steam plough costs £3,000, however, that is the expression in money of *all* the labour embodied in it. Thus, if the machine costs as much as the labour-power it replaces, the human labour embodied in it is always *much less* than that which it replaces. (P. 380 [392].)

As a means of cheapening production, the machine must *cost less labour than it replaces*. But *for capital its value* must be less than *that of the labour-power supplanted by it*. Therefore, machines that do not pay in England may pay in America (*e.g.*, for stonebreaking). Hence, as a result of certain legal restrictions, machines that formerly did not pay for capital may suddenly make their appearance. (Pp. 380-81 [393-94].)

b. Appropriation of Labour-Power Through Machinery

Since machinery itself contains the power driving it, muscular power drops in value. *Labour of women and children;* immediate *increase in the number of wage-labourers* through the enrolling of members of the family who had not previously worked for wages. Thus *the value of the man's labour-power is spread over the labour-power of the whole family, i.e., depreciated.* Now four persons instead of one must perform not only labour, but also *surplus-labour* for capital that one family may live. Thus the *degree* of exploitation is increased together with the *material* of exploitation. (P. 383 [395].)

Formerly the sale and purchase of labour-power was a relation between *free persons;* now *minors or children* are bought; the worker now sells wife and child—he becomes a *slave-dealer.* Examples (pp. 384-85 [396-97]).

Physical deterioration—mortality of workers' children (p. 386 [397-98]), in industrialised agriculture as well. (Gang system.) (P. 387 [399].)

Moral degradation. (P. 389 [399].) Educational clauses and manufacturers' resistance to them. (P. 390 [399-400].)

The entrance of women and children into the factory finally breaks down the *male worker's resistance to the despotism of capital.* (P. 391 [402].)

If machinery *shortens* the labour-time necessary to produce an object, in the hands of capital it becomes the most powerful weapon for *lengthening* the working-day *far beyond its normal bounds.* It creates, on the one hand, *new conditions* that enable capital to do so, and on the other, *new motives* for so doing.

Machinery is capable of perpetual motion, and limited only by the weakness and limitations of the assisting human labour-power. The machine that is worn out in seven and a half years, working twenty hours daily, absorbs *just as much surplus-labour* for the capitalist, *b u t i n h a l f t h e t i m e,* as another that is worn out in fifteen years working ten hours daily. (P. 393 [404].)

The moral depreciation of the machine—by superseding—is in this way risked still less. (P. 394 [404-05].)

Moreover, a larger quantity of labour is absorbed *without increasing the investments* in buildings and machines; thus not only does surplus-value grow with a lengthened working-day, but the outlay required to obtain it diminishes relatively. This is more important in so far as the proportion of *fixed* capital greatly predominates, as is the case in large-scale industry. (P. 395 [405].)

During the first period of machinery, when it possesses a *monopoly* character, profits are enormous, and hence the thirst for more, for boundless lengthening of the working-day. With the general introduction of machinery this monopoly profit vanishes, and the law asserts itself that surplus-value arises, not from the labour *supplanted* by the machine, but from the labour *employed* by it, that is, from the variable capital. But under machine production the latter is necessarily *reduced* by the large outlays. Thus there is an irherent contradiction in the capitalist employment of machinery: for a given mass of capital it *increases* one factor of surplus-value, its *rate*, by *reducing* the other, the number of workers. As soon as the value of a machine-made commodity becomes the regulating social value of that commodity, this contradiction comes to light, and *again drives towards lengthening the working-day*. (P. 397 [407].)

But at the same time machinery, by setting free supplanted workers, as well as by enrolling women and children, produces a *surplus working population*, which must let capital dictate the law to it. Hence machinery overthrows all the moral and natural bounds of the working-day. Hence the paradox that the most powerful means of shortening labour-time is the most infallible means of converting the whole lifetime of the worker and of his family into available labour-time for expanding the value of capital. (P. 398 [408].)

We have already seen how the social reaction occurs here through the fixing of the normal working-day; on this basis there now develops the *intensification of labour*. (P. 399 [409].)

At the beginning, with the speeding-up of the machine, the intensity of labour increases simultaneously with the lengthening of labour-time. But soon the point is reached where the two exclude each other. It is different, however, when labour-time is restricted. Intensity can only grow; in 10 hours as much work can be done as ordinarily in 12 or more, and now the more intensive working-day counts as *raised to a higher power*, and labour is measured not merely by its time, but by its intensity. (P. 400 [409].) Thus, in 5 hours of necessary and 5 hours of surplus-labour, the same surplus-value can be attained as in 6 hours of necessary and 6 hours of surplus-labour at lower intensity. (P. 400 [410].)

How is labour intensified? In *m a n u f a c t u r e* it has been proved (Note 159, p. 401 [411, footnote 1]), pottery, for instance, etc., that *mere shortening of the working-day* is sufficient to raise productivity enormously. In *machine labour* this was far more doubtful. But R. Gardner's proof. (Pp. 401-02 [411-12].)

As soon as the shortened working-day becomes *law*, the machine becomes a means of squeezing more intensive labour out of the worker, either by greater speed or fewer hands in relation to machine. Examples. (Pp. 403-07 [412-16].) Evidence that enrichment and expansion of the factory grew simultaneously therewith. (Pp. 407-09 [416-18].)

c. The Whole Factory in Its Classical Form

In the factory the *machine* takes care of the proper manipulation of the tool; thus the qualitative differences of labour developed in manufacture are here abolished; labour is *levelled out* more and more; at most, difference in age and sex. The division of labour is here a *distribution of workers among the specialised machines.* Here division is only between *principal workers,* who are really employed at the tool, and *feeders* (this is true only for the self-acting mule, scarcely so for the throstle, and still less for the corrected power loom), in addition, supervisors, engineers and stockers, mechanics, joiners, etc., a class only outwardly aggregated to the factory. (Pp. 411-12 [420].)

The necessity for adapting the worker to the continuous motion of an automaton requires training from childhood, but by no means that a worker be any longer chained to one detail function all his life, as in manufacture. Change of personnel can take place at the same machine (relay system), and because of the slight effort required to learn, the workers can be shifted from one kind of machine to another. The work of the attendants is either very simple or is taken over more and more by the machine. None the less, at the beginning, manufacture division of labour persists traditionally, and itself becomes a greater weapon for exploitation by capital. The worker becomes a lifelong part of a detail machine. (P. 413 [422-23].)

All capitalist production, in so far as it is not only a labour process but also a process for expanding the value of capital, has this in common that it is not the worker who employs the instruments of labour, but *vice versa, the instruments of labour employ the worker*; but only through machinery does this perversion acquire technical, *palpable reality*. Through its conversion into an *automaton*, the instrument of labour *itself confronts the labourer*, during the labour process, *as capital*, as dead labour that dominates and sucks dry the living labour-power. Ditto the intellectual powers of the production process as the power of capital over labour.... The detail skill of the individual, pumped-out machine operator vanishes as a tiny secondary thing alongside science, the tremendous natural forces and social mass labour which are embodied in the machine system. (Pp. 414, 415 [423].)

Barracks-like discipline of the factory, factory code (P. 416 [423-24].)

Material conditions of the factory. (Pp. 417-18 [425-27].)

c' or d. The Workers' Struggle Against
the Factory System and Machinery

This struggle, existing since the origin of the capitalist relationship, first occurs here as a revolt against the machine as the material basis of the capitalist mode of production. Ribbon looms. (P. 419 [427-28].) Luddites. (P. 420 [428-29].) Only later do the workers distinguish between the material means of production and the social form of their exploitation.

In manufacture the improved division of labour was rather a means of *virtually* replacing the labourers. (P. 421 [429].) (Digression on agriculture, displacement p. 422 [430].) But in machinery the worker is *actually displaced*; the machine competes with him directly. Hand-loom weavers. (P. 423 [431].) Likewise India. (P. 424 [432].) This effect is permanent, since machinery continually seizes upon new fields of production. The self-dependent and estranged form that capitalist production gives the instrument of labour as against the labourer is developed by *machinery* into a thorough *antagon-*

ism–hence now the labourer's revolt first against the instrument of labour. (P. 424 [432].)

Details of the displacement of workers by machines. (Pp. 425, 426 [433, 435].) The machine as a means of breaking the workers' resistance to capital by displacing them. (Pp. 427, 428 [435-37].)

Liberal economics maintains that the machine, displacing workers, at the same time releases capital that can employ these workers. On the contrary, however, every introduction of machines *locks up* capital, diminishes its *variable* and increases its constant components; it can, therefore, merely *restrict* capital's capacity for employment. In fact–and this is what these apologists also mean–in this manner not capital is set free; but *the means of subsistence* of the displaced workers are set free; *the workers are cut off from the means of subsistence,* which the apologist expresses by saying that *the machine liberates means of subsistence for the worker.* (Pp. 429-30 [438-39].)

This further developed (*very good for Fortnightly*) (pp. 431-32 [439-41]): the antagonisms inseparable from the capitalist employment of machinery *do not exist for the apologists, because they do not arise out of machinery as such, but out of its capitalist employment.* (P. 432 [441].)

Expansion of production by machines directly and indirectly, and thus *possible increase* in number of workers hitherto employed: miners, slaves in cotton states, etc. On the other hand, displacement of Scotch and Irish by sheep to suit the requirements of the woollen factories. (Pp. 433, 434 [443, 444].)

Machine production carries the *social* division of labour much further than manufacture did. (P. 435 [444].)

c″ or e. Machinery and Surplus-Value

The first result of machinery: *increasing surplus-value* together with the mass of products in which it is embodied and on which the capitalist class and its hangers-on live, thus increasing the number of capitalists; new luxury wants together with the means of satisfying them. *Luxury production* grows. Likewise *means of communication* (which, however, absorb only little labour-power in the more developed countries) (evidence p. 436 [445])–finally, the *servant class* grows, the *modern domestic slaves,* whose material is supplied by the *releasing* [of workers]. (P. 437 [446].) *Statistics.*

Economic contradictions. (P. 437 [446].)

Possibility of *absolute increase* in the mass of labour in one branch of business owing to machines, and the modalities of this process. (Pp. 439-40 [449].)

Enormous elasticity, capacity for sudden extension of large-scale industry to a high degree of development. (P. 441 [450-51].) Reaction upon the *countries producing raw materials.* Emigration owing to release of workers. International division of labour of the industrial and agricultural countries–periodicity of crises and prosperity. (P. 442 [451].) Workers thrown back and forth in this process of expansion. (P. 444 [454].)

Historical data on this. (Pp. 445-49 [455-59].)

Displacement of co-operation and manufacture by machinery (and the intermediate stages, pp. 450-51 [459-60]). Also displacement of establishments not run on factory lines, industry branches in the spirit of large-scale industry–domestic industry, an outside department of the factory. (P. 452 [461].) In home industry and modern manufacture, exploitation still more shameless than in the factory proper. (P. 453 [462].) Examples: London print-shops (p. 453 [462-63]), book-binding, rag-sorting (p. 454 [463]), brick-making (p. 455 [463-64].) Modern manufacture in general. (P. 456 [465].) *Domestic industry: lace making* (pp. 457-59 [466-68]), *straw plaiting* (p. 460 [468-69]). Conversion into factory production with achievement of ultimate limit of exploitability: *wearing apparel* by the *sewing-machine* (pp. 462-66 [470-74]). Speeding-up of this conversion by extension of the compulsory Factory Acts, which put an end to the old routine based upon unlimited exploitation. (P. 466 [475].) *Examples: pottery* (p. 467 [475-76]), *lucifer matches* (pp. 468 [476]). Furthermore, effect of the Factory Acts upon irregular work, owing to the workers' irregular habits, as well as to seasons and fashions. (P. 470 [478].) Overwork alongside idleness, owing to the seasons, in domestic industry and manufacture. (P. 471 [478-79].)

Sanitary clauses of the Factory Acts. (P. 473 [480-81].) Educational clauses. (P. 475 [482-83].)

Discharge of workers merely because of *age,* as soon as they are grown up and are no longer fitted for the work, and can no longer live on a child's wages, while at the same time they have learned no new trade. (P. 477 [484-85].)

Dissolution of the *mysteries,* and of the traditional ossification of manufacture and handicraft, by modern industry, which converts the production process into a conscious application of natural forces. Hence it alone is *revolutionary,* as against all earlier forms. (P. 479 [486-87].) But as a capitalist form it lets the ossified division of labour *persist for the worker,* and since it daily revolutionises the former's basis, it ruins the worker. On the other hand, in this very thing, in this necessary change of activities of one and the same worker lies the requirement of his being as versatile as possible and the possibilities of the social revolution. (Pp. 480-81 [487-88].)

Need for extending factory legislation to all branches not operated on factory lines. (P. 482 ff. [489-ff.].) Act of 1867. (P. 485 [493].) Mines, note. (P. 486 ff. [495-503].)

Concentrating effect of the Factory Acts; generalisation of factory production and thus of the classical form of capitalist production; accentuation of its inherent contradictions, maturing of the elements for overturning the old society, and of the elements for forming the new. (Pp. 488-93 [498-503].)

Agriculture. Here release of workers by machines is even more acute. Replacement of the peasant by the wage-labourer. Destruction of rural domestic manufacture. Accentuation of the antithesis between town and country. Dispersion and weakening of the rural labourers, whereas the urban workers become concentrated; hence wages of agricultural workers are reduced down to a minimum. At the same time *robbing of the soil:* the acme of the capitalist mode of production is the undermining of the *sources of all wealth:* the soil and the labourer. (Pp. 493-96 [504-07].)

CHAPTER V

FURTHER INVESTIGATIONS
OF THE PRODUCTION OF SURPLUS-VALUE[1]

---

[1] Here the Manuscript breaks off.—*Ed.*

III
SUPPLEMENT
TO *CAPITAL*,
VOLUME THREE

The third book of *Capital* is receiving many and various interpretations ever since it has been subject to public judgement. It was not to be otherwise expected. In publishing it, what I was chiefly concerned with was to produce as authentic a text as possible, to demonstrate the new results obtained by Marx in Marx's own words as far as possible, to intervene myself only where absolutely unavoidable, and even then to leave the reader in no doubt as to who was talking to him. This has been disapproved; it has been said that I should have converted the material available to me into a systematically written book, *en faire un livre*, as the French say; in other words, sacrifice the authenticity of the text to the reader's convenience. But this was not how I conceived my task. I lacked all justification for such a revision; a man like Marx has the right to be heard himself, to pass on his scientific discoveries to posterity in the full genuineness of his own presentation. Moreover, I had no desire thus to infringe—as it must seem to me—upon the legacy of so preeminent a man; it would have meant to me a breach of faith. And third, it would have been quite useless. For the people who cannot or do not want to read, who, even in Volume I, took more trouble to understand it wrongly than was necessary to understand it correctly—for such people it is altogether useless to put oneself out in any way. But for those who are interested in a real understanding, the original text itself was precisely the most important thing; for them my recasting would have had at most the value of a commentary, and, what is more, a commentary on something unpublished and inaccessible. The original text would have had to be referred to at the first controversy, and at the second and third its publication *in extenso* would have become quite unavoidable.

Such controversies are a matter of course in a work that contains so much that is new, and in a hastily sketched and

partly incomplete first draft, to boot. And here my intervention can be of use: to eliminate difficulties in understanding,
to bring more to the fore important aspects whose significance
is not strikingly enough evident in the text, and to make some
important additions to the text written in 1865 to fit the state
of affairs in 1895. Indeed, there are already two points which
seem to me to require a brief discussion.

I

LAW OF VALUE AND RATE OF PROFIT

It was to be expected that the solution of the apparent
contradiction between these two factors would lead to debates
just as much after, as before, the publication of Marx's text.
Some were prepared for a complete miracle, and find themselves disappointed because they see a simple, rational, pro-
saically-sober solution of the contradiction instead of the
hocus-pocus they had expected. Most joyfully disappointed of
course is the well-known, illustrious Loria. He has at last found
the Archimedian fulcrum from which even a gnome of his
calibre can lift the solidly built gigantic Marxian structure
into the air and explode it. What! He declaims indignantly.
Is that supposed to be a solution? That is pure mystification!
When the economists speak of value, they mean value that is
actually established in exchange. "No economist with any
trace of sense has ever concerned himself with or will ever want
to concern himself with a value which commodities do not
sell for *and never can sell for (ne possono vendersi mai)* ...
In asserting that the value for which commodities *never* sell
is proportional to the labour they contain, what does Marx do
except repeat in an inverted form the thesis of the orthodox
economists, that the value for which commodities sell is *not*
proportional to the labour expended on them?... Matters are
not helped by Marx's saying that despite the divergency of
individual prices from individual values the total price of all
commodities always coincides with their total value, or the
amount of labour contained in the totality of the commodities.
For inasmuch as value is nothing more than the exchange ratio
between one commodity and another, the very concept of a
total value is an absurdity, nonsense... *a contradictio in adjecto....*" At the very beginning of the book he argues, Marx

says that exchange can equate two commodities only by virtue of a similar and equally large element contained in them, namely, the equal amount of labour. And now he most solemnly repudiates himself by asserting that commodities exchange with one another in a totally different ratio than that of the amount of labour contained in them. "Was there ever such an utter *reductio ad absurdum*, such complete theoretical bankruptcy? Was ever scientific suicide committed with greater pomp and more solemnity!" (*Nuova Antologia*, Feb. 1, 1895, pp. 478-79.)

We see: our Loria is more than happy. Wasn't he right in treating Marx as one of his own, as an ordinary charlatan? There you see it—Marx sneers at his public just like Loria; he lives on mystifications just like the most insignificant Italian professor of economics. But, whereas Dulcamara[1] can afford that because he knows his trade, the clumsy Northerner, Marx, commits nothing but ineptitudes, writes nonsense and absurdities, so that there is nothing left finally for him but solemn suicide.

Let us save for later the statement that commodities have never been sold, nor can ever be sold, at the values determined by labour. Let us deal here merely with Mr. Loria's assurance that "value is nothing more than the exchange ratio between one commodity and another", and that therefore "the very concept of a total value of commodities is an absurdity, nonsense... a *contradictio in adjecto*". The ratio in which two commodities are exchanged for each other, their value, is therefore something purely accidental, stuck on to the commodities from the outside, which can be one thing today and something else tomorrow. Whether a metric hundredweight of wheat is exchanged for a gramme or a kilogramme of gold does not in the least depend upon conditions inherent in that wheat or gold, but upon circumstances totally foreign to both. For otherwise these conditions would also have to assert themselves in the exchange, dominate the latter on the whole, and also have an independent existence apart from exchange, so that one could speak of a total value of commodities. That is nonsense, says the illustrious Loria. No matter in what ratio two commodities may be exchanged for each other, that is their value—and that's

---

[1] Charlatan in *L'Elisir d'Amore*, comic opera by Donizetti.—*Ed.*

all there is to it. Hence value is identical with price, and every commodity has as many values as the prices it can get. And price is determined by supply and demand; and any one asking any more questions is a fool to expect an answer. But there is a little hitch to the matter. In the normal state, supply and demand balance. Therefore, let us divide all the commodities in the world into two halves, the supply group and the equally large demand group. Let us assume that each represents a price of 1,000 billion marks, francs, pounds sterling, or what you will. According to elementary arithmetic that makes a price or value of 2,000 billions. Nonsense, absurd, says Mr. Loria. The two groups together may represent a price of 2,000 billions. But it is otherwise with value. If we say price: 1,000+1,000=2,000. But if we say value: 1,000+1,000=0. At least in this case, where the totality of commodities is involved. For here the commodities of each of the two groups are worth 1,000 billion only because each of the two can and will give this sum for the commodities of the other. But if we unite the totality of the commodities of the two in the hands of a third person, the first has no value in his hand any longer, nor the second, and the third certainly not—in the end no one has anything. And again we marvel at the superiority with which our southern Cagliostro has manhandled the concept of value in such a fashion that not the slightest trace of it has been left. This is the acme of vulgar economics![1]

---

[1] Somewhat later, the same gentleman "well-known through his fame" (to use Heine's phrase) also felt himself compelled to reply to my preface to Volume III—after it was published in Italian in the first number of *Rassegna* in 1895. The reply is printed in the *Riforma Sociale* of February 25, 1895. After having lavished upon me the inevitable (and therefore doubly repulsive) adulation, he states that he never thought of filching for himself Marx's credit for the materialist conception of history. He acknowledged it as early as 1885—to wit, quite incidentally in a magazine article. But in return he passes over it in silence all the more stubbornly precisely where it is due, that is, in his book on the subject, where Marx is mentioned for the first time on page 129, and then merely in connection with small landed property in France. And now he bravely declares that Marx is not at all the originator of this theory; if Aristotle had not already suggested it, Harrington undoubtedly proclaimed it as early as 1656, and it had been developed by a Pleiad of historians, politicians, jurists and economists long before Marx. All of which is to be read in the French edition of Loria's book. In short the perfect plagiarist. After I

In Braun's *Archiv für soziale Gesetzgebung*, Vol. VII, No. 4, Werner Sombart gives an outline of the Marxian system which, taken all in all, is excellent. It is the first time that a German university professor succeeds on the whole in seeing in Marx's writings what Marx really says, stating that the criticism of the Marxian system cannot consist of a refutation—"let the political careerist deal with that"—but merely in a further development. Sombart, too, deals with our subject, as is to be expected. He investigates the importance of value in the Marxian system, and arrives at the following results: Value is not manifest in the exchange relation of capitalistically produced commodities; it does not live in the consciousness of the agents of capitalist production; it is not an empirical, but a mental, a logical fact; the concept of value in its material definiteness in Marx is nothing but the economic

---

have made it impossible for him to brag any more with plagiarisms from Marx, he boldly maintains that Marx adorns himself with borrowed plumes just as he himself does.

Of my other attacks, Loria takes up the one concerning his assertion that Marx never planned to write a second or indeed a third volume of *Capital*. "And now Engels replies triumphantly by throwing the second and third volumes at me ... excellent! And I am so pleased with these volumes, to which I owe so much intellectual enjoyment, that never was a victory so dear to me as today this defeat is—if it really is a defeat. But is it actually? Is it really true that Marx wrote, with the intention of publication, this mixture of disconnected notes that Engels, with pious friendship, has compiled? Is it really permissible to assume that Marx ... confided the coronation of his work and his system to these pages? Is it indeed certain that Marx would have published that chapter òn the average rate of profit, in which the solution, promised for so many years, is reduced to the most dismal mystification, to the most vulgar playing with phrases? It is at least permissible to doubt it.... That proves, it seems to me, that Marx, after publishing his magnificent (*splendido*) book, did not intend to provide it with a successor, or else wanted to leave the completion of the gigantic work to his heirs, outside his own responsibility."

So it was written on p. 267. Heine could not speak any more contemptuously of his philistine German public than in the words: "The author finally gets used to his public as if it were a reasonable being". What must the illustrious Loria think his public is?

In conclusion, another load of praise comes pouring down on my unlucky self. In this our Sganarelle puts himself on a par with Balaam, who came to curse but whose lips bubbled forth "words of blessing and love" against his will. For the good Balaam was distinguished by the fact that he rode upon an ass that was more intelligent than its master. This time Balaam evidently left his ass at home.

expression for the fact of the social productive power of labour as the basis of economic existence; in the final analysis the law of value dominates economic processes in a capitalist economic system, and for this economic system quite generally has the following content: the value of commodities is the specific and historical form in which the productive power of labour, in the last analysis dominating all economic processes, asserts itself as a determining factor. So says Sombart, it cannot be said that this conception of the significance of the law of value for the capitalist form of production is wrong. But it does seem to me to be too broad, and susceptible of a narrower, more precise formulation; in my opinion it by no means exhausts the entire significance of the law of value for the economic stages of society's development dominated by this law.

There is a likewise excellent article by Conrad Schmidt on the third volume of *Capital* in Braun's *Sozialpolitisches Zentralblatt*, February 25, 1895, No. 22. Especially to be emphasised here is the proof of how the Marxian derivation of average profit from surplus-value for the first time gives an answer to the question not even posed by economics up to now: how the magnitude of this average rate of profit is determined, and how it comes about that it is, say, 10 or 15 per cent and not 50 or 100 per cent. Since we know that the surplus-value first appropriated by the industrial capitalist is the sole and exclusive source from which profit and rent flow, this question solves itself. This passage of Schmidt's article might be directly written for economists *à la* Loria, if it were not labour in vain to open the eyes of those who do not want to see.

Schmidt, too, has his formal misgivings regarding the law of value. He calls it a scientific *hypothesis*, set up to explain the actual exchange process, which proves to be the necessary theoretical starting point, illuminating and indispensable, even in respect of the phenomena of competitive prices which seem in absolute contradiction to it. According to him, without the law of value all theoretical insight into the economic machinery of capitalist reality ceases. And in a private letter that he permits me to quote, Schmidt declares the law of value within the capitalist form of production to be a pure, although theoretically necessary, fiction. This view, however, is quite incorrect in my opinion. The law of value has a far greater and more definite significance for capitalist production than that of a mere hypothesis, not to mention a fiction, even though a necessary one.

Sombart as well as Schmidt—I mention the illustrious Loria merely as an amusing vulgar-economic foil—does not make sufficient allowance for the fact that we are dealing here not only with a purely logical process, but with a historical process and its explanatory reflection in thought, the logical pursuance of its inner connections.

The decisive passage is to be found in Marx, Vol. III, p. 200:

"The whole difficulty arises from the fact that commodities are not exchanged simply as *commodities*, but as *products of capitals*, which claim participation in the total amount of surplus-value, proportional to their magnitude, or equal if they are of equal magnitude."

To illustrate this difference, it is supposed that the workers are in possession of their means of production, that they work on the average for equally long periods of time and with equal intensity, and exchange their commodities with one another directly. Then, in one day, two workers would have added by their labour an equal amount of new value to their products, but the product of each would have different value, depending on the labour already embodied in the means of production. This latter part of the value would represent the constant capital of capitalist economy, while that part of the newly-added value employed for the worker's means of subsistence would represent the variable capital, and the portion of the new value still remaining would represent the surplus-value, which in this case would belong to the worker. Thus, after deducting the amount to replace the "constant" part of value only advanced by them, both workers would get equal values; but the ratio of the part representing surplus-value to the value of the means of production—which would correspond to the capitalist rate of profit—would be different in each case. But since each of them gets the value of the means of production replaced through the exchange, this would be a wholly immaterial circumstance.

"The exchange of commodities at their values, or approximately at their values, thus requires a *much lower stage* than their exchange at their prices of production, which requires a definite level of capitalist development.... Apart from the domination of prices and price movement by the law of value, it is quite appropriate to regard the values of commodities as not only *theoretically* but also *historically* antecedent (*prius*) to the prices of production. This applies to conditions *in which the labourer owns his means of production,* and this is the condition of the landowning working farmer and the craftsman, in the ancient as well as in the modern world. This agrees also with the view we expressed previously, that the evolution of products into commodities arises through exchange between different communities, not between the members of the same community. It holds not only for this primitive condition, but also for subsequent conditions, based on slavery and serfdom, and for the guild organisation of handicrafts, so long as the means of production involved in each branch of production can be transferred from one sphere to another only with difficulty and therefore the various spheres of production are related to one another, within certain limits, as foreign countries or communist communities." (Marx, Vol. III, I, p. 202.)

Had Marx had an opportunity to go over the third volume once more, he would doubtless have extended this passage considerably. As it stands it gives only a sketchy outline of what is to be said on the point in question. Let us therefore examine it somewhat closer.

We all know that at the beginnings of society products are consumed by the producers themselves, and that these producers are spontaneously organised, in more or less communistic communities; that the exchange of the surplus of these products with strangers, which ushers in the conversion of products into commodities, is of a later date; that it takes place at first only between individual communities of different tribes, but later also prevails within the community, and contributes considerably to the latter's dissolution into bigger or smaller family groups. But even after this dissolution, the exchanging family heads remain working peasants, who produce almost all they require with the aid of their families on their own farmsteads, and get only a slight portion of the required necessities from the outside in exchange for surplus products of their own. The family is engaged not only in agriculture and livestock-raising; it also works their products up into finished articles of consumption; now and then it even does its own milling with the hand-mill; it bakes bread, spins, dyes, weaves flax and wool, tans leather, builds and repairs wooden buildings, makes tools and utensils, and not infrequently does joinery and blacksmithing; so that the family or family group is in the main self-sufficient.

The little that such a family had to obtain by barter or buy from outsiders, even up to the beginning of the nineteenth century in Germany, consisted principally of the objects of handicraft production, that is, such things the nature of whose manufacture was by no means unknown to the peasant, and which he did not produce himself only because he lacked the raw material or because the purchased article was much better or very much cheaper. Hence the peasant of the Middle Ages knew fairly accurately the labour-time required for the manufacture of the articles obtained by him in barter. The smith and the cartwright of the village worked under his eyes; likewise the tailor and shoemaker, who in my youth still paid their visits to our Rhine peasants, one after another, turning the home-made materials into shoes and clothing. The peasants, as well as the people from whom they bought, were themselves workers; the exchanged articles were each one's own products. What had they expended in making these products? Labour and labour alone: to replace tools, to produce the raw material, and to process it they spent nothing but their own labour-power; how then could they exchange these products of theirs for those of other labouring producers otherwise than in the ratio of the labour expended on them? Not only was the labour-time spent on these products the only suitable measure for the quantitative determination of the values to be exchanged: no other was at all possible. Or is it believed that the peasant and the artisan were so stupid as to give up the product of ten hours' labour of one person for that of a single hour's labour of another? No other exchange is possible in the whole period of peasant natural economy than that in which the exchanged quantities of commodities tend to be measured more and more according to the amounts of labour embodied in them. From the moment money penetrates into this mode of economy, the tendency towards adaptation to the law of value (in the Marxian formulation, *nota bene!*) grows more pronounced on the one hand, while on the other it is already interrupted by the interference of usurers' capital and fleecing by taxation; the periods for which prices, on the average, approach to within a negligible margin of values begin to grow longer.

The same holds good for exchange between peasant products and those of the urban artisans. At the beginning this barter takes place directly, without the medium of the merchant, on the cities' market days, when the peasant sells and makes his purchases. Here too, not only does the peasant know the artisan's working conditions, but the latter knows those of the peasant as well. For the artisan is himself still a bit of a peasant; he not only has a vegetable and fruit garden, but very often also has a small piece of land, one or two cows, pigs, poultry, etc. People in the Middle Ages were thus able to check up with considerable accuracy on each other's production costs for raw material, auxiliary material, and labour-time—at least in respect of articles of daily general use.

But how, in this barter on the basis of the quantity of labour, was the latter to be calculated, even if only indirectly and relatively, for products requiring a longer labour, interrupted at irregular intervals and uncertain in yield—grain or cattle, for example? And among people, to boot, who could not calculate? Obviously only by means of a lengthy process of zigzag approximation, often feeling the way here and there in the dark, and, as is usual, learning only through mistakes. But each one's necessity for covering his outlay on the whole always helped to return to the right direction; and the small number of kinds of articles in circulation, as well as the often century-long stable nature of their production, facilitated the attaining of this goal. And that it by no means took so long for the relative amount of value of these products to be fixed fairly closely is already proved by the fact that cattle, the commodity for which this appears to be most difficult because of the long time of production of the individual head, became the first rather generally accepted money commodity. To accomplish this, the value of cattle, its exchange ratio to a large number of other commodities, must already have attained a relatively unusual stabilisation, acknowledged without contradiction in the territories of many tribes. And the people of that time were certainly clever enough—both the cattlebreeders and their customers—not to give away the labour-time expended by them without an equivalent in barter. On the contrary, the closer people are to the primitive state of commodity production—the Russians and Orientals for example—the more time do they still waste today, in order to squeeze out, through long tenacious bargaining, the full compensation for their labour-time expended on a product.

Starting with this determination of value by labour-time, the whole of commodity production developed, and with it the multifarious relations in which the various aspects of the law of value assert themselves, as described in the first part of Vol. I of *Capital*; that is, in particular, the conditions under which labour alone is value-creating. These are conditions which assert themselves without entering the consciousness of the participants and can themselves be abstracted from daily practice only through laborious theoretical investigation; which act, therefore, like natural laws, as Marx proved to follow necessarily from the nature of commodity production. The most important and most incisive advance was the transition to metallic money, the consequence of which, however, was that the determination of value by labour-time was no longer visible upon the surface of commodity exchange. From the practical point of view, money became the decisive measure of value, all the more as the commodities entering trade became more varied, the more they came from distant countries, and the less, therefore, the labour-time necessary for their production could be checked. Money itself usually came first from foreign parts; even when precious metals were obtained within the country, the peasant and artisan were partly unable to estimate approximately the labour employed therein, and partly their own consciousness of the value-measuring property of labour had been fairly well dimmed by the habit of reckoning with money; in the popular mind money began to represent absolute value.

In a word: the Marxian law of value holds generally, as far as economic laws are valid at all, for the whole period of simple commodity production, that is, up to the time when the latter suffers a modification through the appearance of the capitalist form of production. Up to that time prices gravitate towards the values fixed according to the Marxian law and oscillate around those values, so that the more fully simple commodity production develops, the more the average prices over long periods uninterrupted by external violent disturbances coincide with values within a negligible margin. Thus the Marxian law of value has general economic validity for a period lasting from the beginning of exchange, which transforms products into commodities, down to the fifteenth century of the present era. But the exchange of commodities dates from a time before all written history, which in Egypt goes back to at least 2500 B.C., and perhaps 5000 B.C., and in Babylon to 4000 B.C., perhaps 6000 B.C.; thus the law of value has prevailed during a period of from five to seven thousand years. And now let us admire the thoroughness of Mr. Loria, who calls the value generally and directly valid during this period a value at which commodities are never sold nor can ever be sold, and with which no economist having a spark of common sense would ever occupy himself!

We have not spoken of the merchant up to now. We could save the consideration of his intervention for now, when we pass to the transformation of simple into capitalist commodity production. The merchant was the revolutionary element in this society where everything else was stable, stable, as it were, through inheritance; where the peasant obtained not only his hide of land but his status as a freehold proprietor,· as a free or enthralled quit-rent peasant or serf, and the urban artisan his trade and his guild privileges by inheritance and almost inalienably, and each of them, in addition, his customers, his market, as well as his skill, trained from childhood for the inherited craft. Into this world then entered the merchant with whom its revolution was to start. But not as a conscious revolutionary; on the contrary, as flesh of its flesh, bone of its bone. The merchant of the Middle Ages was by no means an individualist; he was essentially an associate like all his contemporaries. The mark association, grown out of primitive communism, prevailed in the countryside. Each peasant originally had an equal hide, with equal pieces of land of each quality, and a corresponding, equal share in the rights of the mark. After the mark had become a closed association and no new hides were allocated any longer, subdivision of the hides occurred through inheritance, etc., with corresponding subdivisions of the common rights in the mark; but the full hide remained the unit, so that there were half, quarter and eighth-hides with half, quarter and eighth-rights in the mark. All later productive associations, particularly the guilds in the cities, whose statutes were nothing but the application of the mark constitution to a craft privilege instead of to a restricted area of land, followed the pattern of the mark association. The central point of the whole organisation was the equal participation of every member in the privileges and produce assured to the guild, as is strikingly expressed in the 1527 license of the Elberfeld and Barmen yarn trade. (Thun: *Industrie am Niederrhein*, Vol. II, 164 ff.) The same holds true of the mine guilds, where each share participated equally and was also divisible, together with its rights and obligations, like the hide of the mark member. And the same holds good in no less degree of the merchant companies, which initiated overseas trade. The Venetians and the Genoese in the harbour of Alexandria or Constantinople, each "nation" in its own *fondaco*–dwelling, inn, warehouse, exhibition and salesrooms, together with central offices–formed complete trade associations; they were closed to competitors and customers; they sold at prices fixed among themselves; their commodities had a definite quality guaranteed by public inspection and often by a stamp; they deliberated in common on the prices to be paid by the natives for their products, etc. Nor did the Hanseatic merchants act otherwise on the German Bridge (*Tydske Bryggen*) in Bergen, Norway; the same held true of their Dutch and English competitors. Woe to the man who sold under the price or bought above the price! The boycott that struck him meant at that time inevitable ruin, not counting the direct penalties imposed by the association upon the guilty. And even closer associations were founded for definite purposes, such as the Maona of Genoa in the fourteenth and fifteenth centuries, for years the ruler of the alum mines of Phocaea in Asia Minor, as well as of the Island of Chios; furthermore the great Ravensberg Trading Company, which dealt with Italy and Spain since the end of the fourteenth century, founding branches in those countries; the German company of the Augsburgers: Fugger, Welser, Vöhlin, Höchstetter, etc.; that of the Nürnbergers: Hirschvogel and others, which participated with a capital of 66,000 ducats and three ships in the 1505-06 Portuguese expedition to India, making a net profit of 150 per cent, according to others 175 per cent (Heyd: *Levantehandel*, Vol. II, p. 524); and a large number of other companies, "Monopolia", over which Luther waxes so indignant.

Here for the first time we meet with a profit and a rate of profit. The merchant's efforts are deliberately and consciously aimed at making this rate of profit equal for all participants. The Venetians in the Levant, and the Hanseatics in the North, each paid the same prices for his commodities as his neighbour; his transport charges were the same, he got the same prices for his goods and bought return cargo for the same prices as every other merchant of his "nation". Thus the rate of profit was equal for all. In the big trading companies the allocation of profit *pro rata* of the paid-in capital share is as much a matter of course as the participation in mark rights *pro rata* of the entitled hide share, or as the mining profit *pro rata* of the mining share. The equal rate of profit, which in its fully developed form is one of the final results of capitalist production, thus manifests itself here in its simplest form as one of the points from which capital started historically, as a direct offshoot in fact of the mark association, which in turn is a direct offshoot of primitive communism.

This original rate of profit was necessarily very high. The business was very risky, not only because of widespread piracy; the competing nations also permitted themselves all sorts of acts of violence when the opportunity arose; finally, sales and marketing conditions were based upon licenses granted by foreign princes, which were broken or revoked often enough. Hence the profit had to include a high insurance premium. Then turnover was slow, the handling of transactions protracted, and in the best periods, which, admittedly, were seldom of long duration, the business was a monopoly trade with monopoly profit. The very high interest rates prevailing at the time, which always had to be lower on the whole than the percentage of usual commercial profit, also prove that the rate of profit was on the average very high.

But this high rate of profit, equal for all participants and obtained through joint labour of the community, held only locally within the associations, that is, in this case the "nation", Venetians, Genoese, Hanseatics, and Dutchmen each had a special rate of profit, and at the beginning more or less for each individual market area,.as well. Equalisation of these different company profit rates took place in the opposite way, through competition. First, the profit rates of the different markets for one and the same nation. If Alexandria offered more profit for Venetian goods than Cyprus, Constantinople or Trebizond, the Venetians would start more capital moving towards Alexandria, withdrawing it from trade with the other markets. Then the gradual equalisation of profit rates among the different nations, exporting the same or similar goods to the same markets, had to follow, and some of these nations were very often squeezed to the wall and disappeared from the scene. But this process was being continually interrupted by political events, just as all Levantine trade collapsed owing to the Mongolian and Turkish invasions; the great geographic-commercial discoveries after 1492 only accelerated this decline and then made it final.

The sudden expansion of the market area that followed and the revolution in communications connected with it, introduced no essential change at first in the nature of trade operations. At the beginning, co-operative companies also dominated trade with India and America. But in the first place, bigger nations stood behind these companies. In trade with America, the whole of great united Spain took the place of the Catalonians trading with the Levant; alongside it two great countries like England and France; and even Holland and Portugal, the smallest, were still at least as large and strong as Venice, the greatest and strongest trading nation of the preceding period. This gave the travelling merchant, the merchant adventurer of the sixteenth and seventeenth centuries, a backing that made the company, which protected its companions with arms also, more and more superfluous, and its expenses an outright burden. Moreover, the wealth in a single hand grew considerably faster, so that single merchants soon could invest as large sums in an enterprise as formerly an entire company. The trading companies, wherever still existent, were usually converted into armed corporations, which conquered and monopolistically exploit- ed whole newly discovered countries under the protection and the sovereignty of the mother country. But the more colonies were founded in the new areas, largely by the state, the more did company trade recede before that of the in- dividual merchant, and the equalisation of the profit rate became therewith more and more a matter of competition exclusively.

Up to now we have become acquainted with a rate of profit only for merchant capital. For only merchant and usurers' capital had existed up to that time; industrial capital was yet to be developed. Production was still predominantly in the hands of workers owning their own means of production, whose work therefore yielded no surplus-value to any capital. If they had to surrender a part of the product to third parties without compensation, it was in the form of tribute to feudal lords. Merchant capital, therefore, could only make its profit, at least at the beginning, out of the foreign buyers of domestic products, or the domestic buyers of foreign products; only toward the end of this period—for Italy, that is, with the decline of Levantine trade—were foreign competition and the difficulty of marketing able to compel the handicraft producers of export commodities to sell the commodity under its value to the exporting merchant. And thus we find here that commodities are sold at their values, on the average, in the domestic retail trade of individual producers with one another, but, for the reasons given, not in international trade as a rule. Quite the opposite of the present-day world, where the production prices hold good in international and wholesale trade, while the formation of prices in urban retail trade is governed by quite other rates of profit. So that the meat of an ox, for example, experiences today a greater rise in price on its way from the London wholesaler to the individual London consumer than from the wholesaler in Chicago, including transport, to the London wholesaler.

The instrument that gradually brought about this revolution in price formation was industrial capital. Rudiments of the latter had been formed as early as the Middle Ages, in three fields—shipping, mining and textiles. Shipping on the scale practised by the Italian and Hanseatic maritime republics was impossible without sailors, i.e., wage-labourers (whose wage relationship may have been concealed under association forms with profit-sharing), or without oarsmen—wage-labourers or slaves—for the galleys of that day. The guilds in the ore mines, originally associated workers, had already been converted in almost every case into stock companies for exploiting the deposits by means of wage-labourers. And in the textile industry the merchant had begun to place the little master-weaver directly in his service, by supplying him with yarn and having it made into cloth for his account in return for a fixed wage, in short, by himself changing from a mere buyer into a so-called *contractor*.

Here we have the first beginnings of the formation of capitalist surplus-value. We can ignore the mining guilds as closed monopoly corporations. With regard to the ship-owners it is obvious that their profit had to be at least as high as the customary one in the country, plus an extra increment for insurance, depreciation of ships, etc. But how were matters with the textile contractors, who first brought commodities, directly manufactured for capitalist account, into the market and into competition with the commodities of the same sort made for handicraft account?

Merchant capital's rate of profit was at hand to start with. Likewise, it had already been equalised to an approximate average rate, at least for the locality in question. Now what could induce the merchant to take on the extra business of a contractor? Only one thing: the prospect of greater profit at the same selling price as the others. And he had this prospect. By taking the little master into his service, he broke through the traditional bonds of production within which the producer sold his finished product and nothing else. The merchant capitalist bought the labour-power, which still owned its production instruments but no longer the raw material. By thus guaranteeing the weaver regular employment, he could depress the weaver's wage to such a degree that a part of the labour-time furnished remained unpaid for. The contractor thus became an appropriator of surplus-value over and above his commercial profit. Admittedly, he had to employ additional capital to buy yarn, etc., and leave it in the weaver's hands until the article for which he formerly had to pay the full price only upon purchasing it, was finished. But, in the first place, he had already used extra capital in most cases for advances to the weaver, who as a rule submitted to the new production conditions only under the pressure of debt. And secondly, apart from that, the calculation took the following form:

Assume that our merchant operates his export business with a capital of 30,000 ducats, sequins, pounds sterling or whatever is the case. Of that, say 10,000 are engaged in the purchase of domestic goods, whereas 20,000 are used in the overseas market. Say, the capital is turned over once in two years. Annual turnover=15,000. Now our merchant wants to become a contractor, to have cloth woven for his own account. How much additional capital must he invest? Let us assume that the production time of the piece of cloth, such as he sells, averages two months, which is certainly very high. Let us further assume that he has to pay for everything in cash. Hence he must advance enough capital to supply his weavers with yarn for two months. Since his turnover is 15,000 a year he buys cloth for 2,500 in two months. Let us say that 2,000 of that represents the value of yarn, and 500 weavers' wages; then our merchant requires an additional capital of 2,000. We assume that the surplus-value he appropriates from the weaver by the new method totals only 5 per cent of the value of the cloth, which constitutes the certainly very modest surplus-value rate of 25 per cent.

$$(2,000 \quad c+500 \quad v+125 \quad s; \quad s'=\frac{125}{500}=25\%, \quad p'=\frac{125}{2,500}=5\%.)$$

Our man then makes an extra profit of 750 on his annual turnover of 15,000, and has thus got his additional capital back in $2^2/_3$ years.

But in order to accelerate his sales and hence his turnover, thus making the same profit with the same capital in a shorter period of time, and hence a greater profit in the same time, he will donate a small portion of his surplus-value to the buyer—he will sell cheaper than his competitors. These will also gradually be converted into contractors, and then the extra profit for all of them will be reduced to the ordinary profit, or even to a lower profit on the capital that has been increased for all of them. The equality of the profit rate is re-established, although possibly on another level, by a part of the surplus-value made at home being turned over to the foreign buyers.

The next step in the subjugation of industry by capital takes place through the introduction of manufacture. This, too, enables the manufacturer, who is most often his own export trader in the seventeenth and eighteenth centuries—generally in Germany down to 1850, and still today here and there—to produce cheaper than his old-fashioned competitor, the handicraftsman. The same process is repeated; the surplus-value appropriated by the manufacturing capitalist enables him (or the export merchant who shares with him) to sell cheaper than his competitors, until the general introduction of the new mode of production, when equalisation again takes place. The already existing mercantile rate of profit, even if it is levelled out only locally, remains the Procrustean bed in which the excessive industrial surplus-value is lopped off without mercy.

If manufacture sprung ahead by cheapening its products, this is even more true of modern industry, which forces the production costs of commodities lower and lower through its repeated revolutions in production, relentlessly eliminating all former modes of production. It is large-scale industry, too, that thus finally conquers the domestic market for capital, puts an end to the small-scale production and natural economy of the self-sufficient peasant family, eliminates direct exchange between small producers, and places the entire nation in the service of capital. Likewise, it equalises the profit rate of the different commercial and industrial branches of business into *one* general rate of profit, and finally ensures industry the position of power due to it in this equalisation by eliminating most of the obstacles formerly hindering the transfer of capital from one branch to another. Thereby the conversion of values into production prices is accomplished for all exchange as a whole. This conversion therefore proceeds according to objective laws, without the consciousness or the intent of the participants. Theoretically there is no difficulty at all in the fact that competition reduces to the general level profits which exceed the general rate, thus again depriving the first industrial appropriator of the surplus-value exceeding the average. All the more so in practice, however, for the spheres of production with excessive surplus-value, with high variable and low constant capital, *i.e.*, with low capital composition, are by their very nature the ones that are last and least completely subjected to capitalist production, especially agriculture. On the other hand, the rise of production prices above commodity values, which is required to raise the below-average surplus-value, contained in the products of the spheres of high capital composition, to the level of the average rate of profit, appears to be extremely difficult theoretically, but is soonest and most easily effected in practice, as we have seen. For when commodities of this class are first produced capitalistically and enter capitalist commerce, they compete with commodities of the same nature produced by pre-capitalist methods and hence dearer. Thus, even if the capitalist producer renounces a part of the surplus-value, he can still obtain the rate of profit prevailing in his locality, which originally had no direct connection with surplus-value because it had arisen from merchant capital long before there was any capitalist production at all, and therefore before an industrial rate of profit was possible.

II

THE STOCK EXCHANGE

1. The position of the stock exchange in capitalist production in general is clear from Vol. III, Part 5, especially Chapter XXVII. But since 1865, when the book was written, a change has taken place which today assigns a considerably increased and constantly growing role to the stock exchange, and which, as it develops, tends to concentrate all production, industrial as well as agricultural, and all commerce, the means of communication as well as the functions of exchange, in the hands of stock exchange operators, so that the stock exchange becomes the most prominent representative of capitalist production itself.

2. In 1865 the stock exchange was still a *secondary* element in the capitalist system. Government bonds represented the bulk of exchange securities, and even their sum-total was still relatively small. Besides, there were joint-stock banks, predominant on the continent and in America, and just beginning to absorb the aristocratic private banks in England, but still relatively insignificant *en masse*. Railway shares were still comparatively weak compared to the present time. There were still only few directly productive establishments in stock company form—and, like the banks, most of all in the *poorer* countries: Germany, Austria, America, etc. The "minister's eye" was still an unconquered superstition.

At that time, the stock exchange was still a place where the capitalists took away each other's accumulated capital, and which directly concerned the workers only as a new proof of the demoralising general effect of capitalist economy and as a confirmation of the Calvinist doctrine that predestination (alias chance) decides, even in this life, blessedness and damnation, wealth, *i.e.*, enjoyment and power, and poverty, *i.e.*, privation and servitude.

3. Now it is otherwise. Since the crisis of 1866 accumulation has proceeded with ever-increasing rapidity, so that in no industrial country, least of all in England, could the expansion of production keep up with that of accumulation, or the accumulation of the individual capitalist be completely utilised in the enlargement of his own business; English cotton industry as early as 1845; the railway swindles. But with this accumulation the number of *rentiers*, people who were fed up with the regular tension in business and therefore wanted merely to amuse themselves or to follow a mild pursuit as directors or governors of companies, also rose. And third, in order to facilitate the investment of this mass floating around as money capital, new legal forms of limited liability companies were established wherever that had not yet been done, and the liability of the shareholder, formerly unlimited, was also reduced ± [more or less] (joint-stock companies in Germany, 1890. Subscription 40 per cent!).

4. Thereafter, gradual conversion of industry into stock companies. One branch after another suffers this fate. First iron, where giant plants are now necessary (before that, mines, where not already organised on shares). Then the chemical industry, likewise machinery plants. On the continent, the textile industry; in England, only in a few areas in Lancashire (Oldham Spinning Mill, Burnley Weaving Mill, etc., tailor co-operatives, but this is only a preliminary stage which will again fall into the masters' hands at the next crisis), breweries (the American ones sold a few years ago to English capital, then Guinness, Bass, Allsopp). Then the trusts, which create gigantic enterprises under common management (such as United Alkali). The ordinary individual firm is more and more only a preliminary stage to bring the business to the point where it is big enough to be "founded".

Likewise in trade: Leafs, Parsons, Morleys, Morrison, Dillon—all founded. The same in retail stores by now, and not merely under the cloak of co-operation *à la* "stores".

Likewise banks and other credit establishments even in England. A tremendous number of new banks, all shares delimited. Even old banks like Glyn's, etc., are converted, with seven private shareholders, into limited companies.

5. The same in the field of agriculture. The enormously expanded banks, especially in Germany under all sorts of bureaucratic names, more and more the holders of mortgages; with their shares the actual higher ownership of landed property is transferred to the stock exchange, and this is even more true when the farms fall into the creditors' hands. Here the agricultural revolution of prairie cultivation is very impressive; if it continues, the time can be foreseen when England's and France's land will also be in the hands of the stock exchange.

6. Now all foreign investments in the forms of shares. To mention England alone: American railways, North and South (consult the stock exchange list), Goldberger, etc.

7. Then colonisation. Today this is purely a subsidiary of the stock exchange, in whose interests the European powers divided Africa a few years ago, and the French conquered Tunis and Tonkin. Africa leased directly to companies (Niger, South Africa, German South-West and German East Africa), and Mashonaland and Natal seized by Rhodes for the stock exchange.

Appendix

INSERTION IN CHAPTER XXVII, *CAPITAL*, BOOK III[1]

Since Marx wrote the above, new forms of industrial enterprises have developed, as we know, representing the second and third degree of stock companies. The daily growing speed with which production may be enlarged in all fields of large-scale industry today, is offset by the ever-greater slowness with which the market for these increased products expands. What the former turns out in months, can scarcely be absorbed by the latter in years. Add to this the protective tariff policy, by which every industrial country shuts itself off from all others, particularly from England, and even artificially increases domestic production capacity. The results are a general chronic overproduction, depressed prices, falling and even wholly disappearing profits; in short, the old boasted freedom

---

[1] Engels's insertion concurs with the description of the role of joint-stock companies and the process of their expansion given by Marx. —*Ed.*

of competition has reached the end of its tether and must itself announce its obvious, scandalous bankruptcy. And in every country this is taking place through the big industrialists of a certain branch joining in a cartel for the regulation of production. A committee fixes the quantity to be produced by each establishment and is the final authority for distributing the incoming orders. Occasionally even international cartels were established, as between the English and German iron industries. But even this form of association in production did not suffice. The antagonism of interests between the individual firms broke through it only too often, restoring competition. This led in some branches, where the scale of production permitted, to the concentration of the entire production of that branch of industry in one big joint-stock company under single management. This has been repeatedly effected in America; in Europe the biggest example so far is the United Alkali Trust, which has brought all British alkali production into the hands of a single business firm. The former owners of the more than thirty individual plants have received shares for the appraised value of their entire establishments, totalling about five million pounds sterling, which represent the fixed capital of the trust. The technical management remains in the same hands as before, but business control is concentrated in the hands of the general management. The floating capital, totalling about one million pounds, was offered to the public for subscription. The total capital is, therefore, six million pounds sterling. Thus, in this branch, which forms the basis of the whole chemical industry, competition has been replaced by monopoly in England, and the road has been paved, most gratifying, for future expropriation by the whole of society, the nation.

NAME INDEX